CARE, CLEANING and SPORTSMANSHIP

M/Sgt. JIM OWENS
USMC (Ret.)

JAFEICA Publishing
Enterprise, Alabama

Copyright ©2015 Jim Owens
All Rights Reserved

ISBN 978-1-939812-85-8

Also available as an ebook for:
- Kindle
- iBooks
- Nook
- Kobo

Visit our website at:
www.jarheadtop.com

Cover image:
Courtesy of Armémuseum (The Swedish Army Museum)
www.digitaltmuseum.se

Chapter heading image by
MatthiasKabel at the German language Wikipedia

Produced by
LOOSE CANNON ENTERPRISES
Paradise, CA
www.loose-cannon.com

DEDICATION

Another Little Giant

This book is dedicated to that special breed of shooters collectively known as "The Juniors." They are special people indeed; they are the future of our sport. They take instructions well and put forth an effort that puts most adults to shame. They are young and have good eyes (I hate 'em).

At Camp Perry in 1998, a couple of juniors made the local papers, the internet forums and were the talk of the Camp when they were caught cheating and sent home in disgrace. I thought you should see the other side of the coin and hear of one of the "Other 98." Her name is Kelly Kasper.

The first time I saw Kelly, she was 13 years old, sitting at the front table on the right side at my High Power class in Green Bay, Wis. I think her feet were swinging because they didn't touch the floor yet. Later that summer she started shooting an AR-15 Service Rifle (it appeared just slightly larger than she was).

When she was 14 years old, at the Camp Perry Fund Match in Eau Claire, Wis. She had just finished a 200-yard sitting rapid-fire string. I came walking down the line and asked "How did you do, Kelly?" She replied in a little girl's forlorn voice "Not as well as I wanted too." "That's not what I asked; how did you shoot?" Again in a forlorn voice she said "Oh, I only had a 98." Bearing in mind there where a hundred people with loaded rifles and knowing what they would have done to me, I resisted the urge to drop kick her.

14 years old and she's shooting High Master scores on rapid fire. So how come she's still a Sharpshooter? Later that day I

asked, "How are your Off-Hand scores?" She said she shoots in the 160's Off-Hand. I looked around for her Dad to ask permission to give her some coaching advice. He was in the pits but I knew Paul would say OK, so we sat on the grassy hillside and I gave her a five-step program to practice in her Off-Hand. I told her "If you do these five steps, you will be shooting in the 180's in six weeks at the Service Rifle Championship."

Three or four weeks later, I asked her "Have you been practicing the five steps?" "Oh, yes, the trigger control exercise has really helped." "What about the sub-six hold?" She sheepishly said, "Well, no." "You dumb shit, you have to do all of the exercises." A few weeks later she had a 91 Off-Hand in the Team Match and a 180 Off-Hand in the Individual Match.

I was coaching four members of our State Service Rifle Team and two targets down Kelly had just finished for the day. I asked how she had shot. When she told me, I turned around and summoned the four guys over and said "I don't want to embarrass you, but I can't help myself." This 14 year old girl just tied our high shooter and beat the other three. I didn't realize how quiet it could get on a rifle range.

During the team match at Camp Perry, again she was two targets down. She had a 99-3x on her 300-yard rapid fire. There was a range alibi and she had to borrow some ammo. On the re-fire she shot a 99-4x.

One day in the pits on Rodriguez Range, a thunder-storm was rolling through. I asked Joe Brown "Where is your rain gear?" "On the 200 yard line" he said. A couple of targets down there was Kelly starting to shiver. I asked "Where is your rain gear you dumb shit?" "On the 200 yard line" she said. "Do you know what you are getting right now?" I asked. She shook her head no. "Experience" I said. I had an extra poncho, so...

Kelly had just turned 15 and her Dad told me she had just got her Master Card. She had gone from Sharpshooter to Master, skipping Expert all together. That was wonderful news. I shook her hand and asked, "Now are you going for Distinguished?" She smiled shyly and said "Well, uh, I ..." "The answer is YES," I said in a stern voice. She squared her shoulders, pulled in her chin and said "YES." Kelly has since shot a 198 at 600 yards and she placed in the "Leg" Match at Camp Perry with a score of 478. She's on her way. Update: She, her Dad and her Brother are all now Distinguished.

When all the negative talk was going around Camp Perry about the two juniors who were caught cheating, it didn't phase me in the least. I remembered a "Little Giant," with a shy smile that has earned all of our respect.

Special Thanks To:

Charlie Milazzo - who was going to write this book...in 1997! But when only ten pages appeared after three months of "writing"... It became apparent that if this book were ever to reach print—Well many hours of conversations converted from Milazzo techno-talk to Owenisms and we were off and running. However, without Charlie this book would never have come to be.

Mike Bykowski - who spent more hours sharing his AR expertise than I had any right to expect, but most surely appreciate (You will too because he can't afford to spend that much time with every caller!) Mike's famous quote: "Clean lightly; clean often."

Boots Obermeyer - for all of the technical knowledge he lent to the Question/Answer section of Chapter 5.

Jack Krieger -who, like Charlie, Mike and Boots, fielded the questionnaire in Chapter 5 and confirmed and re-affirmed their opinions...save one. Jack's famous quote: "I'm not a slave to cleaning!"

Jon Wilcox - for his assistance with Moly-coating info for Chapter 4, legal advice in general and editing assistance.

Tom Krueger - for his editing skills. For all of the grammar errors you find in this book, don't blame Tom. He tried to show me the error of my ways. But the corrected works just don't sound like me!

(All of you readers should thank Jon and Tom... this book would have been 7 long sentences...each chapter beginning with a capital letter and ending with a period.)

Rick Jerry - Owner of Sharpshooter's Supply & Services Ltd. of Green Bay for his info regarding care and cleaning. Chapter 6 of this book is his complete article.

<u>Lee (the) Walker</u> - proprietor of Lee Walker Business Services, for his skills in taking my various bits and pieces of edited information and arranging them in readable sequential pagination. He's what a publishing GURU must be!

<u>Collectively</u> - Dave Hickey, Grant Ubl, Dave Emary and countless other wonderful people (*you know who you are; insert your name here* _____) who lent technical assistance in Chapter 4.

<u>The Seven National Champions</u> who agreed to spend time being interviewed for Appendix A. They're really *COOL* folks. Next time you see one of them at Camp Perry (or your neighborhood Piggly Wiggly) stop and say "Howdy".

My wife of 41 years, Robbie passed away in Oct. of 2004. In 2013 at 70 years young I married a wonderful lady. Corrie now takes good care of me and spoils both me and our dog Toby.

Table of Contents

Foreword   11

Chapter 1   17
Safety, Soft as Steel, Lands & Grooves. Twist rate, Barrel Life, How to break in a Barrel, The Chamber. Head Space Gauge. The Throat. Seating Depth. OAL gauge. The Bullet Comparator. Throat Erosion. The "Sweet Spot." Bullet Run Out. The Crown. Meplat Trimmer.

Chapter 2   59
Always Brush vs NEVER Brush, The Tattle Tale and the Wooden Desk, Bore Tech Eliminator, Horror Stories, Ground Rules for Cleaning the Barrel, The Direction to Clean, Cleaning Rods, Use a Rod Guide, Cleaning Rest, Special Precautions for the M1A, What is the Fundamental - Always Works - Cleaning Routine, Boots' Favorite, How Tight is Tight, The Two Step Scrub Method, M-14 Caution, Get a Rope, Brushing, Getting the Right Size, A Commandment.

Chapter 3   85
Cleaning The AR-15, M-14/M1A Gas System, Marine Corps Magic, The Real Secret, Let's Look Inside, Start a Few Good Habits, Testing for Accuracy, How Often to Break Down and Clean, What Causes the Problem, The Hand Guard, The Stock Ferrule, The Spindle Valve, Grandpa's Farm

Chapter 4   105
Moly Coating, My Learning Process, Electron Microscope, Spray Moly, Moly Snobs, How do you Moly the Bore, Defending the Lady's Honor, Another Method, Removing Moly, My Conclusions on Spray Moly, Powdered Moly, Midways' Kit, Sources of Moly, Do you have to clean the bullets before molying, How do I clean the bore and break in the barrel, What is Kroil and where do you get it, Another cleaning method, A word of Caution, A passing fad.

Chapter 5 135
Questions & Answers

Chapter 6 155
Article by Rick Jerry

Chapter 7 169
Sportsmanship, Have We Given Up, Education, When the Rules Encourage Cheating, What Can You Do, Human Nature, The Little Giant, Susan Smith & Sportsmanship, Teams of Giants.

Appendix A 177
Seven National Champions on Cleaning.

Appendix B 179
Off the Reservation and New Products

Appendix C 197
Source List

About the Author 198

Jim's Shooting Products 200

Foreword

JIM OWENS KNOWS ABSOLUTELY NOTHING ABOUT THE SUBJECT OF "CARE AND CLEANING" OF RIFLES!!!

That's not quite true, I am learning. You probably know as much or more about the subject than I do. Remember, "Everyone has a purpose in life, even if it's just to be used as a bad example." I am the bad example (if Charlie Milazzo died right now, the undertaker would NEVER get the smile off his face).

I'm only telling you this to ward off any claims of my being hypocritical in writing a book on a subject of which I have no knowledge (What a Country). So, how did I get to be so bad? I had formal training from the "blind leading the blind" school of gun care. In 1965 I was taught all the latest techniques, like using a sectional steel rod as a butter churn on my M-14. That might solve the undertaker's problem; Charlie would turn over.

One important thing I learned in my years as a Marine Corps Career Planner is that I didn't have to know every-thing in the thousands of Marine Corps Orders. All I had to know was were to go to find the answer. "Luck is as good as skill, and you don't have to practice." I landed in the geographical center of the best group of people with the greatest wealth of knowledge on the subject at hand. I know where to go to find the answers.

For ten years I gave a high power class in the Milwaukee area. The class went from 7:00 PM — 10:00 PM every Tuesday evening during March and April. Over the nine-week period, I am proud to say, four friends come in as guest instructors: Boots Obermeyer, Jack Krieger, Charlie Milazzo and Mike Bykowski.

How's that for four aces? These gentlemen are the top in their field and are known from coast to coast. In the shooting community, they are legends. You may ask, "I've heard of those two or three, but who is that other guy?" Fair enough question. I'll give you the benefit of the doubt that a) you are new to the sport, b) you don't use the type of rifle associated with that person, or c) word hasn't gotten to your planet yet. For those of you who fall into one of the above categories, I will attempt the impossible, trying to describe these four people in a few paragraphs.

Collectively, Boots Obermeyer and Jack Krieger are two of the best barrel makers in the world. OK, so I'm silly enough to make a flat statement like that and you know several great barrel makers. Many National Championships have been won with either an Obermeyer or Krieger barrel.

Boots and Jack are both super technocrats and nice guys at the same time. They know far more than I can get them to tell in this limited space (the truth is they tell far too much and get too technical). Boots is a firearms expert witness for the State of Wisconsin.

Charlie Milazzo won the Moses look-alike contest. He has been in his workshop so long he hasn't seen daylight since Custer was a Corporal. I would love to recommend him as a gun plumber for the M1A but he gave it up to tinker with his world famous Milazzo AR triggers (what some guys won't do for fame and fortune). Charlie gives the "Care and Cleaning" portion of the Spring Class. He goes into convulsions when I cut him down to two hours. I've learned to never put anything important AFTER his class; the questions and answers alone can last two hours.

Mike Bykowski is that "Other Guy." He is our local celebrity. If you haven't had a Match AR built by Mike, you probably haven't heard of him. About a year ago, I shot an AR built by Mike at 600 yards with my 24-power Leupold scope. I noticed after the first nine shots that seven were in ONE FOURTH of the X ring, from 12 to 3 o'clock. Mike gives the AR portion of the "Care and Cleaning" in the Spring Class. He impressed the hell out of me in last year's class when he said, "If you borrow someone else's AR, you should remove the bolt carrier and inspect it before firing the rifle. If they forgot to put in one important piece; the rifle will fire but the bolt will blow out the back." The tapered pin.

Products and Witches Brews

Joe Blow Smuckatelly says he has this home made "Super Bore Cleaner" and I should tell you about it. Maybe his certain brand of transmission fluid does work beyond belief, but it would be my luck for it to dissolve your barrel overnight. There are hundreds of wonderful products out there. We haven't used or even heard of them all. That's not to say they are not great, there are just too many to recommend. We will give you what we know to be tried and true, and tell you of others that have been recommended. There is a worst case scenario that we will warn you about. The mixing of several products will form a chemical reaction that will dissolve your barrel overnight.

A New Bore Cleaner I Highly Recommend

Henry Ford said, *"if you think you can or if you think you can't, you are right."*

My old spiral-bound books were so out of date and the pictures were so bad I would tell people to take them out to their backyard and burn them.

The other three books have been updated, with better pictures and additional chapters. That was and is my goal for this book. I thought I was close to finishing this book when all of a sudden reality yanked my choker chain.

The technology in the shooting world along with the rest of the world has made great leaps in the rifles, the ammunition and the cleaning products.

My problem was and is some of the products recommended and mentioned in several chapters by friends and experts are no longer what they used to be.

It was and is true that Hoppes will never hurt a barrel. Given enough time it will do its job. The government (EPA) made them remove the one key ingredient that it made it work. Hoppes still smells great, however it is fighting with one hand tied behind its back. I cannot recommend a product I no longer believe in and in several of the chapters Charlie says over and over "Hoppes." So what do I do? I do not want to cut out any of Charlie's information because it is great and he has a world of knowledge.

I was fortunate to come upon a product and company that is truly amazing and it works wonders.

BORE TECH-ELIMINATOR

Eliminator is a bore cleaner that <u>literally wipes-out all copper, lead, carbon, plastic, and powder fouling</u> in minutes instead of hours. Eliminator literally alters the chemical makeup of copper to break its bind from the barrel steel, then uses advanced chelating agents to keep it from re-depositing. <u>Rust preventatives guard against corrosion</u>. Non-toxic, non-flammable, and completely biodegradable. This stuff is incredible!

The Other 98

When I was growing up, a local TV station had a program called "The Other 98." They were referring to the fact that only 2% of the youth were juvenile delinquent, and getting all the attention. The other 98% were the good kids doing fine things.

The 1998 National Rifle Matches at Camp Perry had two juniors caught cheating. They were sent home in disgrace. They were the talk of the town, made the local papers, and were all over the internet.

Right after those two incidents, we had a fund raising dinner to buy shooting equipment for juniors to use while at Camp Perry. We raised $816.00 that night and one of the Camp Perry Officials (Bob Harding, Rodriguez tower talker) matched it with a personal check. Champion's Choice gave us a discount on the equipment and we were able to get four complete sets of shooting gear, everything but a rifle, for the kids.

Care, Cleaning & Sportsmanship

Five juniors from the California team were invited (as our poster children) to raise the needed money. They were well aware of the cheating incidents and it hurt them inside. Talking to these kids helped keep things in perspective for me. I felt pride and respect for them, they represented *the Other 98*.

CHAPTER ONE

I have mixed feelings about safety. Don't get me wrong, I'm one hundred percent for safety. The NRA High Power Competitions program is the safest in the world. Because of the inherent danger, everyone is safety conscious; we police ourselves.

We have all heard a story of some idiot who shot himself or someone else while trying to clean a gun. My circle of friends likes to quote one of the little known items in the fine print of the "Laws of Nature." "Natural Selection" states, "The stupid ones will kill themselves off; hopefully, before they have a chance to breed." I don't like interfering with the laws of nature and that's why I have mixed feelings.

Left to its own devices, the animal kingdom uses natural selection and it works as it should. Man, being an animal that can screw up an anvil with a rubber mallet, throws natural selection akimbo by taking out an innocent bystander before he gets around to killing himself.

Before someone screams about guns in the home for self-defense and the need that they be loaded, I'm not wading into that quicksand. I'm talking about High Power Rifles used for Competition. If you have a rifle at home, or on the range behind the firing line, and it's loaded, you ARE a candidate for "Natural Selection." If you are that stupid and you take yourself out, I personally don't give a damn. But knowing that some people can screw up a good anvil and take out an innocent bystander, I have to interfere by saying "HEY STUPID, unload that rifle before cleaning it. It should never have been loaded off the firing line in the first place."

There is always an exception: **NEWS ITEM, Rifle-cleaning accident kills burglar! ANDERNACH, Germany** - A man was cleaning his rifle when it accidentally discharged - severely wounding a burglar in the apartment above him! Cops say Fritz Grubber's bullet hit the ceiling, passed through the up-stairs floorboards and struck the thief in the groin. "It was a million-to-one shot," says Officer Klaus Schroeder. So much for safety.

Soft as Steel

We think in terms of "As hard as steel." Barrel makers and other technocrats think in terms "as SOFT as steel." Steel can be damaged rather easily. The damage is microscopic and we cannot see the results as they do. If you took a steel plate that had been ground flat and polished smooth, by running your hand over it you might think nothing could damage this. Take a hammer and give it a hard blow to the center of the plate. You won't notice any difference. Let's take a look from the "technocrats" point of view.

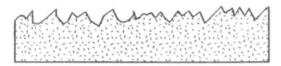

Fig. 1
Cross section of a piece of soft steel that has been ground and polished as the surface would look when viewed using an electron microscope.

Using a large microscope on a cross section of that so-called flat surface, it looks like a mountain range. See Figure 1.

There are peaks and valleys, no matter how much you polish the steel. As this HUGE bullet passes over these tiny peaks they rip off parts of its super-soft copper coating and fill in the valleys. A small amount of this is actually good; it's when large amounts of the copper builds; interfering with the path of the bullet that the problem begins.

The area of our steel plate that was hit with the hammer will show the peaks smashed in and turned over; it is considerably damaged compared to the surrounding area. We can take comfort in the knowledge that not too many tiny men with hammers can fit down our barrel. The point is that the steel can be damaged. There are other things that can, and do, happen on the inside.

Let's look at another and far more common form of damage to our steel plate. On the edge of the plate, take a kitchen carving knife and with only moderate force strike the edge of the plate. Oh, by the way, if you are silly enough to actually do this you are indeed a candidate for natural selection when your wife finds out.

Two types of damage can occur to the edge. One is a cut or "V" shape in the steel. The other, depending on the angle of the blow, is a curl of metal rolled over like a wave in the ocean. When we get to the section on the "Crown" I will explain how these cuts occur and what effects they have on the bullet.

Our soft as steel really gets a workout from some other bad guys: Heat and gases from the fired cartridge; water from humidity causing rust and pitting; abrasive cleaners if used improperly; and, use of different products that cause a chemical reaction that eats into the metal.

Lands & Grooves

In the "Old" days the barrel makers made the bore of the gun smooth, with no lands and grooves. The gun shot just fine but the bullet wasn't very stable and thus not very accurate. By giving the bullet a twist and getting it to rotate in flight, the bullet stabilizes and we have far greater accuracy.

Let's go back to our steel plate. Imagine that a tiny bulldozer has just made a trench down the center of our plate. See Figure 2.

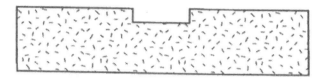

Fig. 2
A groove (trench) cut in the surface of the metal

This is the "Groove." When another groove is cut at a space equal to the width of the groove, the remaining surface between the grooves becomes the "Land." Most people think of the groove as being rather deep. Let's get a perspective and try some mental gymnastics. Look at a ruler and take one inch and mentally divide it into one thousand equal parts. A typical business card is about 12 thousandths of an inch thick. Stand a business card on edge on the ruler and you will start to get the picture. A typical human hair is about three thousandths of an inch thick. Now that you have the perspective let's apply it to the barrel.

The depth of the groove on a .30 cal. barrel is about .004, or four thousandths of an inch. That's just a little deeper than the width of a human hair. On a .223 cal. barrel the depth is only about two and one-half or three thousandths. That really isn't very deep.

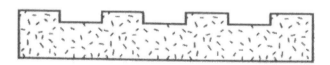

Fig. 3
A series of grooves and lands in a steel plate

In Figure 3, we have made our series of grooves in the steel plate and now we lay a .30 cal. rod down the center and wrap our plate around it, glue it on the edges and we have a barrel. That's the only way I could make a barrel. Charlie says, "Now you know why I'm not a barrel maker."

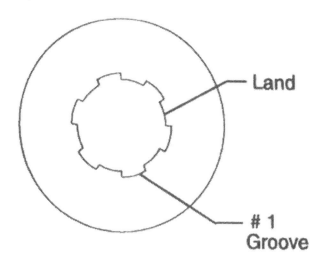

Fig. 4
Cross sectional view of a rifle barrel showing six grooves and six lands

In Figure 4 we look down the bore and land number one is at the six o'clock position all the way down the length of the barrel. It needs a twist to help the bullet rotate and stabilize.

The lands twist like a corkscrew in the barrel. A barrel that has a one in twelve twist means it makes one revolution in twelve inches. A land that starts at the six o'clock position will be at the nine o'clock position after traveling three inches down the barrel. It will be at the twelve o'clock position after traveling six inches down the barrel. Then it will be at the three o'clock position after traveling nine inches. After it has traveled twelve inches it will return to the six o'clock position, and starts all over again. Of course the other lands twist right along with #1.

A barrel that has a 1-11 (one in eleven) twist rotates one time in eleven inches and one with a 1-10 rotates once in ten inches. The lower the number the "Faster" the twist; for example, a 1-9 is faster than a 1-12 twist. **The bullet used MUST be**

compatible with the twist rate. One day during practice on the Marine Corps Rifle Team an "other than normal ammo" was issued for the 200 yard Off-Hand stage. These guys normally fired in the mid to upper 190's; even the ones firing in the low 190's rarely got out of the black.

Mass confusion broke out (yeah, yeah I know, how can you tell with Marines?) when half the shooters were getting eights, sevens and even some six's Off-Hand. Someone thought to ask, "What twist barrel are you shooting?" Some were shooting 1-10 twist and others were shooting 1-12 twist. That was the answer; the 1-12 twist was not compatible with that ammo and it acted like a spoiled child. Some people think they are really bad shooters. In most cases it is simply a matter of getting the right combination.

If you don't know the twist rate of your barrel a simple way to find out is to place a patch on your cleaning rod and insert it about half way down the barrel. Make a mark on the rod at the top or 12 o'clock position. Pull the rod slowly out of the barrel and watch the mark rotate around the rod. When the rod rotates one full revolution and comes back to 12 o'clock, measure the distance from the mark to the end of the barrel. If it is ten inches then you have a one in ten barrel.

A .30 cal. bullet is the diameter of the bullet and it fits nicely between the lands & grooves. If you use a 168 gr. (grain is the weight of the bullet) or a 190 gr. or even a 220 gr. or a .30-cal. they will all fit nicely between the lands. When the bullets are heavier they **can't get fatter**; they have to **get longer**. To shoot the heavier (longer) bullets you must have a faster (lower number) twist to stabilize the bullet and make it compatible with the rifle.

A faster twist will shoot some of the lighter bullets with reasonable accuracy. It is a must for the heavier bullets. A slower twist may be excellent for the lighter bullets, but it will not shoot the heavier ones at all. Bench-Rest shooters are looking for extreme accuracy. High-power shooters want the accuracy, but since they have the different distances to consider, two hundred to one thousand yards, a slightly faster twist would be useful if a heavier bullet was desired. It's all a tradeoff; Err on the side of a faster twist.

Barrel Life versus Accurate Barrel Life

The life of a barrel can be equivalent to the half-life of an atomic bomb target. The barrel may last forever and bullets may still fly down range, but the limit of its accuracy is "It went that-a-way."

The ACCURATE barrel life is what we are concerned with. The number of rounds in an accurate barrel life can and will vary. We'll call this number "X." **Your choice of a barrel, your initial use of a barrel, and your care and cleaning techniques** will determine if the accurate barrel life is X-plus or X-minus.

Your Choice

Barrels are made for different types of shooting; hunting, plinking, competition, etc. Some barrels are made for specific reasons and are given special care and consideration for the type of shooting that will be performed. People use the terms "Quality or Good" barrels, and "Inferior or Bad" barrels. It's all relative. A Formula One racecar and a VW Bug will both get you around the race track. The VW Bug is not a "Bad" car. It all depends on your intended use.

As you shoot a rifle, the gases and unspent powder residue and other crud will cause "fouling" of the barrel. If you are hunting, you don't shoot enough rounds at one time to worry about fouling. If you are shooting bench rest you are concerned with extreme accuracy. So, you take the time to clean the rifle before fouling becomes a problem. In High Power Competition you have to go across the course with 88, or some time with alibis, a hundred or more rounds, without worrying about fouling or loss of accuracy.

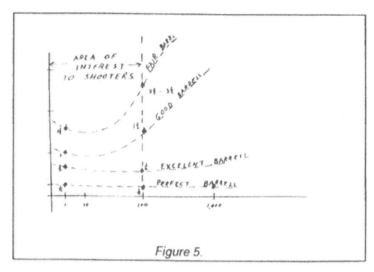

Fig. 5
A graph of a "good" barrel that will hold its accuracy

Figure 5 shows a graph of a "good" barrel that will hold its accuracy (in minutes of angle) for a longer period of time, enough to get you across the course, versus a "poor" barrel designed for other uses. Two of the best are; Obermeyer and Krieger.

Your Initial Use

If you have a "good" quality barrel and would like to see the accurate barrel life be X-plus rather than X-minus, give some consideration to "Breaking in the barrel." I talked to a local Army unit's Marksmanship Instructor. He said, they just got in ten brand new rifles. I ask him, "How do you break in the barrels?" He said, "Oh, we just shoot them." That answer gets an X-minus. Charlie Milazzo gave me the best answer on why you should break in a barrel.

The best elephant joke I ever heard was, "How do you make a statue of an elephant? You take a large block of stone and carve away everything that doesn't LOOK like an elephant!" The barrel maker uses a cutter called a "Reamer" to go inside a steel rod and cut away everything that doesn't look like a barrel. Actually it's a three-step process. First he uses a rough cutter to get the hole, then he uses the reamer to shape the bore, and finally he rifles it to get the lands and grooves.

A reamer is nothing more than a fancy drill bit. It HAS to rotate; it leaves some microscopic scratches that run around the chamber and the bore. The bullet travels across these raised ridges. The barrel maker "Laps" the barrel to remove as much of the ridges as he can. If he had to spend the many hours it would take to break in the barrel and remove the last little bit, the price of the barrel would sky-rocket. If you break in the barrel you are helping the final process. It could mean the difference between "X" and "X - plus" accurate barrel life.

Charlie used an analogy that shows the results. He says if you have a flat surface that has a slightly raised bump to it, filing the bump will remove metal rather quickly until you get down to the flat surface and metal removal is slower. Breaking in the barrel removes these raised bumps and makes the rifle shoot better. Usually a barrel will shoot better after four or five hundred rounds.

On a good quality barrel, you may start with a minute of angle group. It takes some time to break in a new barrel; both the cleaning break-in and the shooting break-in. After a number of rounds the barrel will improve its accuracy, maybe down to one-half minute of angle. Keep in mind the factors: ammo used, the sights, and the shooter's ability. Eventually the accurate barrel life will be reached and it will open up to its original minute of angle groups. With old age and hard use it will go downhill from there.

How Do You Break in a Barrel?

Jack received a letter saying this guy spent thirty hours breaking in his barrel; all of our eyes collectively crossed.

The process is: clean and shoot, clean and shoot, again, again and again. Notice I didn't say shoot and clean. You want to clean the barrel first to remove any shop dust, shipping dust or fairy dust.

Use a coated cleaning rod.

Use a patch, not a brush.

Use an abrasive cleaner such as Remclean or JB Bore cleaner.

Use Hoppes or (BORE TECH-ELIMINATOR) to flush out the abrasive grit prior to the next shot.

Dry patch several times before the next shot.

How much? Mike has the best common sense answer. "Clean the barrel in the first hundred rounds as often as YOU feel comfortable with." Don't use any special bullets such as hand loads for accuracy or heavy bullets. Your regular old practice ammo will do.

Boots recommends cleaning after each round for the first ten shots. Then clean after every two rounds for the next ten shots, then clean after each string for several five round strings. Take along a radio, this will take several hours. Is it worth it? What do you have to compare to if you don't break in the barrel?

The following article on my web site, www.jarheadtop.com is by
Stuart A. Leach a.k.a. "the Colorado Gray Fox"

Modern gun makers have devised a number of ways to create the long tubes of steel with internal spiraling grooves we call rifle barrels. All start with a blank bar of metal; from there divergence in methods and sequence of operations grows quickly. Some barrel makers do all outside machining before boring, reaming and rifling, others do the opposite. Those spiraling grooves are created through cutting, scraping, broaching (a series of cutting edges on one tool) or hydraulically forcing a reverse image tool through the bore. Hammer forging combines outside shaping with internal dimensioning and rifling. Some makers straighten barrels; others are vehemently against this. Lapping with fine abrasives may or may not be done at various stages. Great barrels are produced by all the varied processes.

The finest attention to detail still leaves some minute roughness inside a new barrel. Chambering leaves some roughness in the lead and throat areas. These microscopic grooves, rings, pits and fins tear at the outside of a bullet as it passes by, causing some of the jacket material to remain behind. Successive shots add to this; residues from primer and powder combustion add to the chemically active mix. As a string of shots progresses the deposits build up, creating constrictions and uneven passage of the bullet through the bore. Barrel vibrations become less uniform, and accuracy suffers.

Think of a firearm as a very simple internal combustion engine. The barrel is the cylinder, the bullet is the piston. In this "free piston" engine we use each piston only once, but we expect several thousand functions from the cylinder. Two dissimilar metal surfaces must move past each other at high speed, under great pressure and with little or no lubrication. Careful break-in of the cylinder will enhance accuracy, allow longer accurate strings between cleanings, ease the cleaning process and extend the life of the barrel. Any barrel will benefit from proper break-in, be it the chrome-moly steel tube on a mass produced hunting rifle or the stainless steel product of the finest custom maker.

Break-in is done at the range, and takes a long morning or afternoon. A series of shots is fired, in combination with very thorough cleanings. The objective is to have successive bullets pass by bare steel, acting to wear down microscopic irregularities and impart a final polish to the barrel. The soft metal bullet jacket has an action much like the effect of a leather strop on a straight razor. Minor rigidities which rise above the base surface of the steel are wiped away.

In addition to the rifle and appropriate plain bullet ammunition the following will be needed:

* Padded cradle or vise to hold the rifle
* Cleaning rod guide
* High quality plastic coated cleaning rod
* Bronze bristle brush
* Plastic or boar bristle brush, or bore mop
* Spear or wrap around patch holder
* Ample supply of patches
* Powder solvent such as Hoppe's, Shooters Choice, etc.
* Copper solvent such as Sweet's 7.62, or abrasive cleaner such as JB Bore Paste
* Wiping rags

Before firing the first shot wipe out the barrel with powder solvent and patch dry. Some pretty strange things can get in a barrel during final assembly and shipping, let alone while on a display rack. Firing that first shot without cleaning risks damage to the bore.

Fire one, and only one, shot and clean well with powder solvent, bronze brush and patches. Always use an eye dropper or squeeze bottle to apply the solvent to the brush; dipping the brush in the bottle just contaminates your whole solvent supply. Wipe the rod between passes. Now clean again with copper solvent. Apply the copper solvent with the plastic or boar bristle brush, or with the mop- this stuff eats bronze brush bristles! Apply liberally, and allow to work for three to five minutes. Position the rifle with the muzzle low to keep solvent from draining into the action and bedding. I like to dry fire, shoot another gun, shoot the breeze, etc. while waiting.

The first patch after applying copper solvent will show a lovely azure blue color. This is made up mostly of copper compounds, the products of a chemical reaction between bullet jacket metals and the ammonia in the solvent. Patch dry, apply more copper solvent, wait, and patch again. Repeat this regime until no blue color shows on that first patch. The barrel must be cleaned down to bare steel.

Some custom barrel makers recommend that each shot be fired across clean, dry steel uncontaminated by powder fouling or jacket material. Alternatively, some well-respected bench rest gunsmiths recommend a "wet" break-in, where the barrel is cleaned as described and a light coating of Rem Oil ™, Kroil ™ or a similar light bodied oil is applied before the next shot is fired. Both schools emphasize one shot at a time, and thorough cleaning. Some 'smiths and barrel makers are also endorsing use of the mild abrasive cleaners such as JB Bore Paste, Rem Clean or IOSSO.

Fire another single round, and clean again. Keep this up for at least ten rounds, fifteen would be better. After a few rounds you will find fewer doses of copper solvent are needed to get a clean patch. The break-in process is progressing. A Rocky Mountain Rifle Works (Mark Chanlynn) 30 caliber match barrel needed fewer doses after just five rounds; a Norinco SKS never did need fewer doses.

Finally, fire a series of three shot groups, cleaning as before. After three to five groups and cleanings the break-in process is complete. Shoot well, being confident that you have done your part to enhance barrel performance.

* * *

Here is another great article on the break-in and cleaning by Jack Krieger:

Break-In and Cleaning
by Jack Krieger

BREAK-IN

With any premium barrel that has been finish lapped —such as your Krieger Barrel—, the lay or direction of the finish is in the direction of the bullet travel, so fouling is minimal. This is true of any properly finish-lapped barrel regardless of how it is rifled. If it is not finish-lapped, there will be reamer marks left in the bore that are directly across the direction of the bullet travel. This occurs even in a button-rifled barrel as the button cannot completely iron out these reamer marks.

Because the lay of the finish is in the direction of the bullet travel, very little is done to the bore during break-in, but the throat is another story. When your barrel is chambered, by necessity there are reamer marks left in the throat that are across the lands, i.e. across the direction of the bullet travel. In a new barrel they are very distinct; much like the teeth on a very fine file. When the bullet is forced into the throat, copper dust is released into the gas which at this temperature and pressure is actually a plasma. The copper dust is vaporized in this gas and is carried down the barrel. As the gas expands and cools, the copper comes out of suspension and is deposited in the bore. This makes it appear as if the source of the fouling is the bore when it is actually for the most part the new throat. If this copper is allowed to stay in the bore, and subsequent bullets and deposits are fired over it; copper which adheres well to itself, will build up quickly and may be difficult to remove later. So when we break in a barrel, our goal is to get the throat polished without allowing copper to build up in the bore. This is the reasoning for the "fire-one-shot-and-clean" procedure.

Barrels will vary slightly in how many rounds they take to break in because of things like slightly different machinability of the steel, or steel chemistry, or the condition of the chambering reamer, etc. For example a chrome moly barrel may take longer to break in than stainless steel because it is more abrasion-resistant even though it is the same hardness. Also chrome moly has a little more of an affinity for copper than stainless steel so it will usually show a little more "color" if you are using a chemical cleaner. (Chrome moly and stainless steel are different materials with some things in common and others different.) Rim Fire barrels can take an extremely long time to break in—sometimes requiring several hundred rounds or more. But cleaning can be lengthened to every 25-50 rounds. The break-in procedure and the clearing procedure are really the same except for the frequency. Remember the goal is to get or keep the barrel clean while polishing out the throat.

Finally, the best way to break-in the barrel is to observe when the barrel is broken in; i.e. when the fouling is reduced. This is better than some set number of cycles of "shoot and clean" as many owners report practically no fouling after the first few shots, and more break-in would be pointless. Conversely, if more is required, a set number would not address that either. Besides, cleaning is not a completely benign procedure so it should be done carefully and no more than necessary.

Care, Cleaning & Sportsmanship

CLEANING

This section on cleaning is not intended to be a detailed instruction, but rather to point out a few "do's and don'ts". Instructions furnished with bore cleaners, equipment, etc. should be followed unless they would conflict with these "do's and don'ts."

You should use a good quality straight cleaning rod with a freely rotating handle and a rod guide that fits both your receiver raceway and the rod snugly. How straight and how snug? The object is to make sure the rod cannot touch the bore. With service rifle barrels a good rod and guide set-up is especially important as all the cleaning must be done from the muzzle and even slight damage to the barrel crown is extremely detrimental to accuracy.

There are two basic types of bore cleaner—chemical and abrasive. The chemical cleaners are usually a blend of various ingredients including oils and ammonia that attack the copper. The abrasive cleaners generally contain no chemicals and are an oil, wax, or grease base with an extremely fine abrasive such as chalk, clay, or gypsum. They clean by mechanically removing the fouling. Both are good, and we feel that neither will damage the bore when used properly.

So what is the proper way to use them? First, not all chemical cleaners are compatible with each other. Some, when used together at a certain temperature, can cause severe pitting of the barrel—even stainless steel barrels. It is fine to use two different cleaners as long as you completely remove the first cleaner from the barrel before cleaning with the second. And, of course, never mix them in the same bottle.

Follow instructions on the bottle as far as soak time, etc. Always clean from the breech whenever possible, pushing the patch or swab up to the muzzle and then back without completely exiting the muzzle. If you exit the muzzle, the rod is going to touch the bore and be dragged back in across the crown followed by the patch or brush. Try to avoid dragging things in and out of the muzzle. It will eventually cause uneven wear of the crown. Accuracy will suffer and this can lead you to believe the barrel is shot out, when in fact, it still may have a lot of serviceable life left. A barrel with a worn or damaged crown can be re-crowned and accuracy will usually return.

The chemical cleaners may be the best way to clean service rifle barrels that must be cleaned from the muzzle — i.e. M1 Garand, M14, etc. — because this method avoids all the scrubbing necessary with the abrasive cleaners and the danger of damaging the crown. But again, as long as the rod doesn't touch the crown, abrasive cleaners should be fine.

Abrasive cleaners work very well. They do not damage the bore, they clean all types of fouling (copper powder, lead, plastic), and they have the added advantage of polishing the throat both in "break in" and later on when the throat begins to roughen again from the rounds fired. One national champion we know polishes the throats on his rifles every several hundred rounds or so with diamond paste to extend their accuracy life.

Again, as with the chemical cleaners, a good rod and rod guide is necessary. A jag with a patch wrapped around it works well. Apply the cleaner and begin scrubbing in short, rather fast strokes of about two to four inches in length. Concentrate most of the strokes in the throat area decreasing the number as you go toward the muzzle. Make a few full-length passes while avoiding exiting the muzzle completely, but do partially exit for about six strokes. You can avoid accidentally exiting by mounting the rifle in a vise or holder of some sort and blocking the rod at the muzzle with the wall or something to keep it from completely exiting.

This sheet is intended to touch on the critical areas of break-in and cleaning and is not intended as a complete, step-by-step guide or recommendation of any product.

The following is a guide to "break-in" based on our experience. This is not a hard and fast rule, only a guide. Some barrel, chamber, bullet, primer, powder, pressure, velocity etc. combinations may require more cycles some less!

It is a good idea to just observe what the barrel is telling you with its fouling pattern. But once it is broken in, there is no need to continue breaking it in.

Initially you should perform the shoot-one-shot-and-clean cycle for five cycles. If fouling hasn't reduced, fire five more cycles and so on until fouling begins to drop off. At that point shoot three shots before cleaning and observe. If fouling is reduced, fire five shots before cleaning. It is interesting to shoot groups during the three and five shot cycles.

Stainless	Chrome-moly
5 one shot cycles	5-25 one shot cycles
1 three shot cycle	2 three shot cycles
1 five shot cycle	1 five shot cycle

KRIEGER BARRELS, INC.
2024 Mayfield Road, Richfield, WI 53076
PH: 262-628-8558

As far as I'm concerned, if the experts (barrel makers & gunsmiths) recommend it and that's good enough for me.

The Chamber

A rifle's chamber is a marvelous little invention. It is misunderstood and frequently overlooked when it comes to care and cleaning. The chamber is much like a glove; it is shaped like the object that is placed inside. It is a tad larger than its intended object to allow easy entry and removal.

When the bolt is pushed forward, it picks up a cartridge and places it in the chamber. The round fits snugly, waiting to be fired. When you squeeze the trigger, the hammer falls and strikes the firing pin, slamming it into a little detonator called the primer. A tiny but powerful explosion occurs inside the case. In Boot Camp we had a guy who couldn't hit the broad side of a barn from the inside, because he let the stats of the

M-14 freak him out: "50,000 lbs. of force per square inch of chamber pressure."

In high school physics the teacher said, "An airline pilot would rather have an elephant walk down the aisle of his plane rather than a 110 lb. lady in spiked heels." The force is concentrated onto that spike. If the back of that bullet were one square inch, it would have 50,000 lbs. of force pushing it down the barrel. Since the area is so much smaller the amount of force is increased and really pushes the bullet out there.

The part of the force that is thrown back at us is called "recoil." The rest of the force inside the cartridge expands the brass until it grips the side of the chamber walls. The back portion of the brass moves a little more, because of the give in the bolt. The brass is stretched all around, but particularly close to the head. When reloading we squeeze the brass back to a size that will allow it to reenter the chamber. If the reloading die is set too long it will not squeeze the brass enough. If the reloading die is set too short and we over-squeeze the brass, it will fit inside the chamber, but it will stretch more than it should.

Every time we reload, we squeeze the brass down. When we shoot, the chamber pressure expands it out again. This constant "working" of the brass weakens it; the brass becomes hardened and brittle. It must remain springy to do its job. If the brass is sized correctly (the reloading die is set right), it will only expand one or two thousandths of an inch. You will get longer life out of your brass. If not sized right, the brass is overworked. You will get head separations, and/ or the brass won't fit into the chamber properly.

People get head separations after four or five reloads and someone says, "You're reloading your brass too many times." Boots says if your die is set correctly you can get 20 to 30 reloads. **SPECIAL NOTE FOR GAS GUNNERS**, Charlie says it's better to size your brass a little smaller for safety's sake, to help avoid slam fires.

Care, Cleaning & Sportsmanship

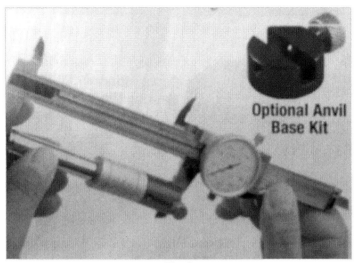

Fig 6
Head Space Gauge

To set your reloading sizing die to the proper depth and to insure you compress the brass correctly, a head space gauge is essential. There are several good ones on the market. Boots recommends Mo's or RCBS. The one by Mo is large and easy to use. The RCBS is a little slower, but has a bullet seat depth gauge. I was one who could screw up that anvil with the rubber mallet until I started using Tom Peterson's Stoney Point Products. He has **a head space gauge** that comes in a little kit (Fig. 6).

Fig. 7

The kit has five bushing sizes that allow use on most bottleneck cases, from .17 Remington through the belted magnums. You don't need a special gauge for each caliber. The bushings fit on the body of his "Bullet Comparator" (You're going to need this any-way) and it fits onto your dial caliper (Fig. 7).

Follow the instructions for the setup of the bushings, measure a case that was fired in your rifle and set the sizing die to one or two thousandths less. It's so easy even I can do it and my brass lasts longer.

A simple way to check to see if a piece of brass is about to separate is to take a piece of wire or a paper clip and bend one end into a small "L" shape. Run the hook down into the brass and you can feel the hairline crack that forms on the inside of the case.

Sam Burkhalter once said that when the walls of the brass expand and grip the chamber, the crack gives way. The head separates and the body of the brass is left, stuck inside the chamber. People panic, start scrambling for a stuck case remover. He recommends if you leave it alone for a minute or two, the chamber will cool, the brass contracts enough that you give the rifle a little tap and the case will fall out. A couple of shooters had a stuck case. By the time I could get down to them with the case remover, I remembered what Sam had said. All I did was pick up the rifle, the case fell into my hand. I handed it to them and walked away. I heard one of them say, "WOW, did you see that?" I smiled and thought, "Luck is as good as skill."

When the primer causes the powder to burn and the bullet is sent down the bore with a lot of gases, crud and spent powder residue go with it. Some crud blows back around the neck of the case and into the chamber. If you fire close to a hundred rounds and don't clean the chamber, it doesn't take long for the crud in the chamber to build up. The problem occurs when the available space in the chamber is decreased and is almost the same size as the case. The cartridge has a hard time going in and coming out.

If you are firing a bolt gun and this problem occurs, the shooter will compensate, subconsciously, by applying more force. Service Rifles cannot apply more force when needed. The spring has just so much strength to bring the op rod and bolt forward. There is a finite amount of gas returned in the system to push that op rod and bolt, and to remove the case from the chamber. You will get failure to feed and failure to extract alibis (remember, only one per stage). The technocrats say it throws the timing off.

The reason the chamber is often overlooked is that people think the patch takes care of the chamber when it cleans the bore. Not true. Get yourself a brass or nylon chamber brush and wrap a patch around it. The M-14 chamber brush has a ratchet on the end and a section of a steel cleaning rod makes an excellent handle.

The Throat

The throat of the barrel is that piece of no man's land between the chamber and the point where the lands and grooves begin. I thought the lands and grooves started right at the chamber; again, oh silly me. One look at the throat of a well-used barrel and you will see why it is so inhospitable. It looks like a sun baked, dry lakebed, cracked and flaky. The tremendous heat and gases from the exploding primer and burning powder brings the metal to a rapid heating. All the surrounding metal, siphoning off the heat, makes for a rapid rate of cooling.

The rapid expansion of the metal from the heat and the rapid contraction of the metal from the cooling puts a lot of stress on that area; no wonder it's like a snake shedding its skin. Many things happen in this area and I could spend a lot of time on it. I like to give useful information, what I call "meat and potatoes" information, something you can use to improve your shooting.

I'm going to give you two useful pieces of information. One is on the proper cleaning of this area. The other is actually some reloading information, as it directly relates to the throat of the barrel.

The cleaning of the throat is accomplished when and (IF) you clean the chamber. Charlie says that the abrasive cleaners are most useful in the early and late stages of a barrel's life. The "early stage" is useful during the break-in period. The "late stages" are when the throat is looking like a dried lakebed. I have heard that Mid Tomkins uses Jewelers Rouge to polish up the throat for longer life of the barrel.

Tom Peterson of Stoney Point Products said the lands and the grooves do not start right at the chamber. There is an area known as "Freebore throat leade." That is the area we novices call the throat.

When loading ammo, if we set the bullet out too long it touches the bore. You can get excessively high pressure and possibly a dangerous condition. Some people do it routinely; then again, some people jump off high bridges attached to a rubber band. The problem occurs when some of the rounds are just off the lands & grooves and others just touch. The high pressure will cause wide shots as compared to the ones not touching the lands. When it comes to High Power Competition, touching the bullet to the lands is like teaching a pig to sing; it wastes your time and it just annoys the pig.

In the old days the conventional wisdom was to have the bullet set only two to five thousandths off the lands. The methods of measuring were like calculating the distance from LA to NY with a yardstick; it can be done, but there are better ways.

The part of the area the bullet has to jump before it reaches the bore and the lands is called "Free-travel clearance jump." I'm going to cut this term down to "freebore" for brevity. **It has been noticed that a particular bullet (any bullet) likes a particular jump (freebore) for a chosen rifle.** Change bullets or change rifles and the freebore most likely will change. Yes, the rifle will still fire and the groups will still be reasonably accurate if you do not have the "Correct" jump. Oh, but once you do get the correct jump, one **THAT** rifle and bullet combination likes, you'll notice the accuracy is incredible. Asking some-one, "How far off the lands do you set your bullets?" does no good. His rifle may like .015, but your rifle may be .020 or .025.

Tom Peterson showed me the method and when I worked up some loads, the results were spectacular. I was using Wayne Anderson's .30 cal. VLD's and I took a load from the reloading manual. All the powder weights and the bullet weights were the same. The only difference was the "**seating depth**" of the bullets.

Per Tom's recommendation I started with a seating depth of ten-thousandths off the lands and went deeper (into the case) by five-thousandths on each five round group. I used a yellow Post-it-note with a three-quarter-inch black paster in the center as a target; each note had the reloading info for each group. Using my bolt gun and 24 power scope, prone position with a sandbag under my left wrist at one hundred yards, I fired several five round groups.

One was the seating depth and/or freebore jump my rifle liked. My reward? The first shot was a half-inch to the right due to a bad call. The second shot was on call. The third shot went through the second hole as did the fourth and fifth. I went home and loaded twenty-two more with the same seating depth. That Saturday at a league match, 200 yards, 600 slow fire reduced, I shot a 200 with 16 X's.

The old yard stick methods of smoking the bullet or marking the cleaning rod just didn't do the job. Mike was nice enough to make a couple of collars that tighten down on my cleaning rod and I could take the measurements between the collars. I got so wrapped up in the numbers that I didn't notice I had a bullet stuck in the lands. It could have been disastrous if I hadn't been able to insert my open bolt indicator. The world needed a better mousetrap.

Fig. 8

To get the desired amount of jump you must have a starting point of reference. You need to know the overall length of your bullets. The problem is the tip of the bullet doesn't touch the lands, it goes up into the bore; it's the ogive that touches the lands and each type of bullet has a different ogive. Tom Peterson has become the "White Knight" of shooters because he came to the rescue with his Stoney Point Products. The OAL (for "Over All Length") gauge is perfect for the job. The straight OAL gauge (Fig.8) is used on bolt guns and AR's where you can remove the bolt and come at the chamber from the rear.

Fig. 9

The curved gauge that will work on the M 1A and M-1 Garand (Fig. 9). The "Modified Case" is screwed onto the OAL gauge.

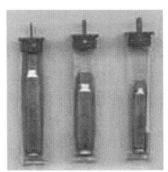

Fig. 10
Modified Case to fit onto the OAL gauge

Place the type bullet you will be using into the slightly expanded neck of the "Modified Case" (Fig. 10).

Set the bullet into the "Modified Case" far deeper than normal and slide the case into the chamber. Slowly push the sliding rod on the OAL gauge forward until you feel the bullet touch the lands, use a wooden dowel to get a precise feel when the bullet touches the lands, give the end of the OAL rod several light taps to ensure the bullet is seated. Now tighten down the thumb screw so the rod stays in place and remove the OAL gauge and bullet for measuring (you must have the bullet for measuring so you can't leave it stuck in the lands; for safety alone, the OAL gauge is worth the price). If the bullet sticks simply tap it out with a wooden dowel and replace it into the "Mod Case"; the thumbscrew holds the correct setting.

Fig. 11 The bullet comparator

Now that you have the overall length you have to measure it to get your reference point. Again in the old days the only way to measure the overall length of a bullet was to measure it from the base or head to the tip of the bullet, with a caliper. I measured ten rounds (loaded at the same time) from base to tip, and came up with up to eight-thousandths variations in length. I took Stoney Point's **<u>Bullet Comparator</u>** (Fig. 11) and measured the same ten rounds (off the Ogive) and came up with only ONE thousandth difference.

The bullet comparator attaches with a thumbscrew to the leg of your dial caliper. It has a set of bushings that measure almost all of the different calibers; the headspace gauge bushings attach to the same comparator body. Once you measure the OAL on the gauge you now have your reference point. Make up a dummy round set to that length. Now make up your test loads in five-thousandths increments deeper seating (giving you a longer jump). You MUST test fire them on the range; there is no other way. You can bench rest them if you like. When you get one the rifle really likes you will be amazed how the size of the group reduces.

Note: The OAL-Straight, The OAL-Curved, The Bullet Comparator, Concentricity Gauge Used to check bullet run out and Competition Seating Die can all be purchased from Sinclair International, 800-717-6211 or Jim Owens 334-347-0020.

WHAT CAN YOU DO?

Pull the rod the OAL gauge entire way back, insert a bullet into the neck of the mod case, and make sure it goes down into the case. Place the case into the chamber and push the rod forward. The rod will push the bullet forward until the bullet touches the lands. Tighten the thumbscrew to hold the rod in place and remove the gauge. If the bullet sticks in the lands, simply tap it out with a cleaning rod, being careful of the barrel's crown. Place the bullet back into the neck and simply measure the overall length from the tip of the bullet to the bottom of the case with a dial caliper.

Remember, this length is where the bullet touches the lands, and this length gives the excessive pressure. You will want to seat the bullet a little deeper into the case, so you set your seating die a few thousandths shorter than this measurement. How much shorter? I read one article that said 3 to 5 thousandths. I tried that and boy did I get in trouble. I made my measurement and set my die for 3 thousandths deeper and started to seat a bunch of bullets. I don't just set the die, take three or four measurements, and then run the batch. I measure every round, and I have found that every seating die I've tried will not seat to an exact amount. They will seat to an acceptable range. Charlie says, "It's not the fault of the die, the bullets do not have uniform tips, the ogives are uniform and that's where measurements should be taken." Tips don't have to be perfect to give good accuracy, but the bases do.

Figure 11 shows a tool made by Tom Peterson called the "bullet comparator" and it attaches to your dial caliper. It measures the **seating depth off the ogive and not the tip.**

When I first got the "Bullet Comparator" I did a little experiment. I had ten (10) .308 loaded rounds, so I used my old method of measuring them with my dial caliper (From the tip of the round to the base). I got .012 thousands variation on the lengths. I then placed the bullet comparator body on the dial caliper and inserted the .308 insert. I then measured the same ten rounds. **The bullet comparator measures off the ogive of the bullet and not the tip.** I got .001 thousand variation from the same ten rounds. I was impressed.

I had one round that would not seat down to the proper depth so I set it aside. At the end of that lot, I set it deeper and kept setting it deeper until it measured the same as the others. I used it as my first sighter and thought my rifle had blown up!! I was lucky it hadn't. Smoke came out of the floor plate; the primer was blown out. I now measure every round and, if it will not seat to within the range I want, it goes in the discard pile.

I use 15-20 thousandths as my free bore, or jump, and it works pretty well. Remember to re-check the overall length after every thousand rounds, more often if you use 220 gr. bullets. As the throat erodes, seat your bullets out to the new length and it will help eliminate those fliers.

Tom Peterson has retired and has sold his business to Hornady. The items above are available from Sinclair International 800-717-8211 or Jim Owens 334-347-0020.

THROAT EROSION

When the bullet leaves the chamber to be hurled down the bore, and rotated by the lands and grooves, it must first jump through the area known as the "Throat." This is a slight taper leading to the lands and grooves. The bullet leaves the neck of the cartridge and makes a "jump" through the throat to engage the lands and grooves.

"The smaller the jump or "Free Bore," the greater the accuracy, and the fewer the fliers." That is not true. Yes, I did write that in the Blue book, but I have learned new information since then.

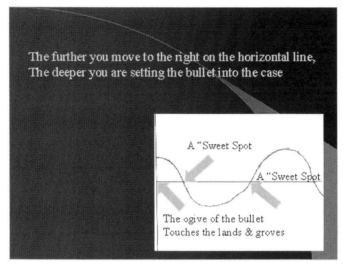

Fig. 12
There is a "Sweet Spot" that will give you the best group.

There is a "Sweet Spot" that must be found (fig. 12), actually there are several "Sweet Spots," one of the sweet spots could be 10 thousands off the lands and a second sweet spot could be forty-thousands off the lands. Once you find one of the sweet spots, your Long Range groups will shrink tremendously.

There can be "More Than One" sweet spot

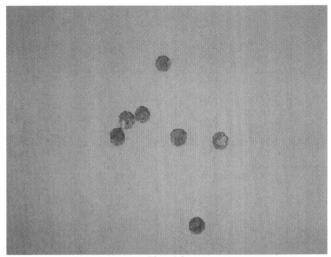

Fig. 13
This 1st picture (Fig. 13) is .005 **before** a sweet spot.

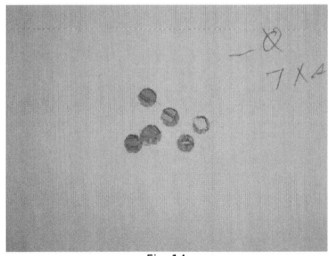

Fig. 14
This 2nd picture (Fig. 14) is **on** the sweet spot.

Care, Cleaning & Sportsmanship

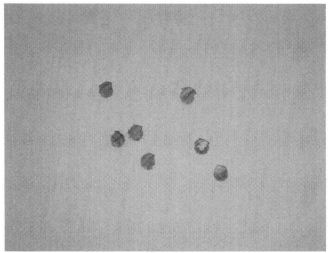

Fig. 15
This 3rd picture (Fig. 15) is .005 **after** the sweet spot.

Update

I have tested this in my Advanced High Power Classes. I have proven there are more than one sweet spot. They seem to be .030 apart.

Charlie gave me a simple explanation of harmonics (I said I wouldn't know a harmonic if it came up and bit me). When the rifle fires, the bullet starts down the bore. The sound wave travels through the metal much faster than the bullet. When the sound waves reach the end of the barrel, they bounce back and returns. The bullet and the sound waves cross over and the sound waves reach the other end and again returns. The bullet and the waves continue to cross. Somehow this makes up the harmonics of the rifle. The "BOSS" compensator on the end of the rifle gives you something to play with to adjust for the harmonics and improve accuracy. You can't have one on the end of your rifle, but you can do the same thing with the seating depth.

To maintain this accuracy you will have to repeat the above procedure after every thousand rounds fired, even sooner if you use a lot of heavy bullets. The hot gases and heavy bullets wear on the throat and make the freebore or jump longer as time goes by. Cleaning out the snake scales is important but having a happy rifle with a correct jump will add to your "Accurate Barrel Life."

In my one week class, I teach you how to find the sweet spot.

You should not have the bullet touch the lands, and have no jump, because this condition can cause excessive or inconsistent pressure. The excessive pressure could be dangerous, and inconsistent pressure is not conducive to optimum accuracy.

The amount of jump, or free bore, in the Rapid Fire stages must be rather large. The bullets are seated into the cartridge necks deep enough to insure: (1) that they will fit into the magazine for the service rifles, and, (2) that they will feed into the well when fed by stripper clips on a bolt rifle. Fortunately, the Rapid Fire stages are held at closer ranges and the problem is not significant.

With a new barrel, that hasn't been broken in, the free bore is rather small. You may start with your bullets set fairly deeply into the cartridge case and there is no problem.

Being fat, dumb and happy, I never knew there was a problem until I talked with Charlie. I thought those fliers were my fault. I found out that as you shoot more and more rounds, the throat wears, and it becomes larger. The more rounds you have fired, the more the bullet has to jump. I also found that using a heavier bullet, something I like to do, causes the throat to wear even faster.

I would like to take a minute and make a public apology to all the Marine Corps Armorers. They were always after me to keep up my yellow book "record of rounds fired" that was issued with each rifle. I never did. Now I know the importance of keeping that record. I now keep a log of my rounds fired in my Data Book (Fig.16), every time I shoot, the number of shots fired is recorded. The *Jim Owens Data Books* have this log in the back of the book. It is a great tool.

Fig. 16

Charlie has taught me that as the throat wears and the bullet has a longer jump, you have to seat your bullets out longer, to reduce the amount of free bore. Most of the rounds will make the jump just fine, but some of the bullets have slight imperfections within the core. As the bullet makes the longer jump, the center of mass is slightly off. This is why you check your bullets when you reload for evenness and roundness. Even though it will go down the barrel spinning, it will not spin on its true axis. It will have a slight "wobble" as it leaves the barrel. As little as a thousand rounds through the rifle can cause enough throat erosion to cause the problem. It can be measured.

BULLET RUN OUT

I started to pay attention to throat erosion and seating depth, but I was still getting fliers. Charlie said, "How about your bullet run out?" I told him, "I may be so ugly, my mother had to tie a pork chop around my neck to get the dog to play with me, but I've never had a bullet run out on me yet." I opened my mouth too soon. Then I found out what bullet run out was.

In the final stages of hand loading, you place a bullet into the neck of the case; run the press up and the die "seats" the bullet. In a perfect world, the bullet would be seated dead center into the neck of the case and, when fired, would rotate on its axis as it goes down the barrel. There would be no wobble. The die seldom seats the bullet dead center. It is off by varying amounts, which can be measured. This is usually the fault of the brass and can be encountered even when using precision seating dies.

A bullet that is really bad may be placed on a flat surface (like a table) and you will see the tip wobble as you roll the case. If the bullet is that bad, you could have a seven or six at 600 yards and think it is your "poor" shooting ability.

Fig. 17 Concentricity Gauge

WHAT ARE YOU WILLING TO ACCEPT?

The shooter who loads his own ammunition without checking for run out, either doesn't know about it or is willing to accept things as they are. We see some shooters who think a six-inch group at 100 yards is just great ("That's the best I've ever shot!"). We know we can do better. Run out becomes important at long ranges, so we have to set a maximum range or maximum run out we will accept. Charlie says, "For national match shooting, no more than six thousandths". My standard is four thousandths.

You have to have a way to check for run out, to know how much you have. Figure 17 is a "Concentricity Gauge" sold by Sinclair International 800-717-8211.

The dial indicator is placed to ride on the bullet at the "Ogive," the part that starts sloping down to the tip. You can rotate the dial until it reads zero or read it from any point on the dial. You are looking for the combined number of thousandths of an inch above and below the starting point. You need to rotate the case rather quickly and watch the needle move.

I got a _real_ education when I tested my hand loads. The ones that had six thousandths run out were my _good_ ones. I was getting 8, 10, 12, and 15 thousandths run out. Someone told me, "If you set the bullet in the neck, run the case one halfway into the die, stop, rotate the case within the shell holder, then finish seating the bullet, it will help." Not enough for my money.

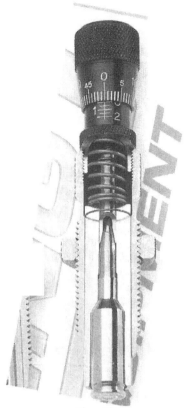

Fig. 18

With the standard seating die I was using, I was getting 50% of my loads at 6-12 thousandths run out—not acceptable. I ordered a "Competition Seating Die" (The kind with a micrometer adjustment on top see fig. 18) and 100% of my loads became within six thousandths or less.

I still check all of my rounds. I find some rounds have zero run out and 1-2 thousandths is common. Any rounds over four thousandths are used for practice or close range.

The Crown

Yes, I know, "Everyone has a purpose in life, even if it's just to be used as a bad example." It does explain the existence of some members of our society. Everything was fine, until I became the bad example for Charlie Milazzo. He cut about two inches off the end of one of my old barrels so he could carry it around in his pocket to show "MY" crown to anyone he could get to stand still long enough. It didn't matter they had no idea what they were looking at, he was having a devilish technocratic glee at my expense. For any of you interested, YES the contract I have out on him is still good.

There's good news and bad news. The bad news is that the crown is the easiest part of a rifle barrel to damage, damage that will affect your accuracy without your knowing about it. The good news is, with some knowledge, a change in your cleaning techniques and some care you can prevent the damage. A crown that has been damaged can be re-crowned for about $25.00 to $60.00.

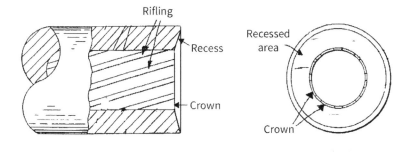

Fig. 19

So, what is the Crown?

Figure 19 shows a side view and an end view of the end of a rifle barrel, or the muzzle. Notice the end is recessed to help protect the crown. Let's use our imagination again. If an ant were crawling down the bore toward the muzzle, to him it would look like a tunnel. When he came to the end there is nothing but empty space, so he goes over the edge and down the face of the muzzle. <u>The edge itself is the crown (Fig.20)</u>. It should be crisp and sharp all the way around the "tunnel."

Fig. 20

Fig. 21

Care, Cleaning & Sportsmanship

When we fire a round, the gases pushing the bullet down the bore will escape in an even pattern as it leaves the muzzle and the undamaged crown. The lands have given the bullet a rotation to stabilize it and the bullet flies true (no wobble).

Mike said he had a customer who took his jointed cleaning rod with a brush and chucked it up in a power drill to REALLY clean the bore (now THAT'S a bad example).

We regular bad examples, who previously used a jointed rod, now know better. If you don't know better, here is what happens. When a jointed (multi-section) rod is screwed together it never fits perfectly. Run your fingers lightly down a rod and you'll notice a slight bump at each of the joints. When those joints hit the crown they do damage by nicking (low technical term) the metal (Fig. 21). You can create several nicks every time you push the rod through.

Remember our knife on the edge of the steel plate? The two types of damage are 1) the "V" cut and 2) the "Roll Over" piece of medal (Fig. 21). The same thing happens to the crown. With the "V" cut, the gases escape unevenly and give the bullet a wobble or yaw. Since there is no more bore or lands to stabilize it, the bullet will not fly true. With the "Rolled Over" piece of medal in the bore, you have a speed bump for bullets. Hit a speed bump with your car at twenty miles per hour and you'll get the idea.

So, I got rid of my jointed rod and got a one piece, coated Dewey or Parker-Hale rod and now I'm no longer a bad example. WRONG! The jag that holds the patches and the adapter both have screw on joints, I now was simply creating fewer dings at a time.

Leave it to me to discover new ways to screw up the anvil with the rubber mallet. Remclean is the old Gold Medallion abrasive bore cleaner and Boots likes it very much. I put some on the patch and while cleaning from the breech of my bolt rifle pushed it down the bore and exited the muzzle, (no one ever told me not to) so I pulled the patch back into the bore and removed it at the back end.

Charlie discovered that by pulling the patch back into the muzzle, I was compressing the patch again and getting a wear spot on the crown at the six o'clock position because of the abrasive cleaner.

He now gets to look like the hero by telling people, "Never exit the barrel with the patch, stop just short and then pull back. If you do exit, take the patch off before carefully pulling the jag past the crown." Playing straight man to a gunsmith is no picnic.

What the hell is a Meplat?

The short answer is, the ragged tip of a hollow point bullet. So, why is it important? Listen up, this is really important.

We had a bolt-gun shooter show up at a match, only to discover he had all his bullets seated out for long range. They were too long to fit in the receiver for rapid fire. He took a flat file and he filed off the tips of the bullets and made the rounds short enough to fit into the receiver. He shot 100-7X.

Another shooter did the same thing by loading his rounds too long. He did not have a file, so he placed each round, one at a time on, the cement and taped the tip of the bullet with a hammer, into the case to make them shorter. He fired a 100-3X.

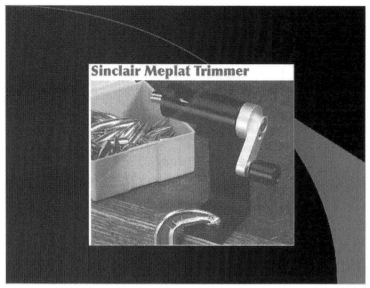

Fig. 22

Nowadays there is a much better way. There is now a tool (fig. 22) that trims the meplat. The funny part is, the advantages are more for Long Range ammo. Actually it works great for 300 yards and at longer distances. It has little or no affect at 200 yards or shorter. In fact the further back you shoot the better it works.

The advantages are: 1) the groups are smaller and rounder, anywhere from 15% to 45% smaller than the non-trimmed bullets. Also, trimmed bullets have less flyers.

This sounds too good to be true. I had a class with 10 students so I decided to see for myself. I had each of the 10 people shoot a 10 shot string with the untrimmed bullets and another 10 shot string with the trimmed bullets. I had them do this both at 300 yards and again at 600 yards.

I took each person's data book and I accurately plotted each string before trimming and after trimming, again at both 300 yards and again at 600 yards. Guess what — it works as advertised. The groups with the trimmed bullets were smaller and rounder. Some were about 10% to 15% smaller and some groups were about 40% to 45% smaller.

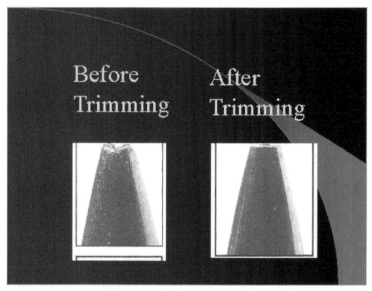

Fig. 23

The tips of the bullets look like someone had cut them off with a meat cleaver (Fig 23). The tool itself can use different inserts for the caliper you want to use. See the before and after pictures.

Okay, where can I get this wonder tool? Once again Sinclair International 260-493-7104 or Jim Owens 334-347-0020.

Keep in mind, this works on hollow point bullets. It does not work for the plastic tip ones like the A-Max bullets.

Between getting the correct seating depth to find your "Sweet Spot" and trimming the meplat's, you will have a huge advantage over the other shooters at 300 yards through 1000 yards.

CHAPTER TWO

Always Brush vs. NEVER Brush

Lee Trevino said, "If ever I'm on a golf course during a thunder storm, I'm going to hold a one iron straight up in the air. Even God can't hit a <u>one</u> iron." I'm not about to test that theory. A person can control the "odds" of risk. Stay inside on a beautiful day and the odds of your being struck by lightning are extremely low. Go outside on that same beautiful day and the odds are still extremely low. Go out in a thunderstorm and the odds go up. They go up even more if you're on a golf course standing under a tree. Hold a one iron straight up in that thunderstorm and God will not be able to resist the temptation to prove Lee Trevino wrong.

Damage to the "Crown" while cleaning the barrel is like being struck by lightning, there is a real risk of which to be aware, except that the possibility of damage is already extremely high. Brushing while cleaning makes the odds even higher. Standing around talking to your friends and not paying attention while you brush is like holding up a "one" iron.

I received a letter from a shooter, and he wrote that some people at his club tell him to always use a brush when cleaning and others tell him to never use a brush when cleaning the barrel. "Which is true?" The answer is, "Neither." There are tradeoffs and other factors involved: time and money. Another letter asked "What is the best, sure-fire method of cleaning a barrel." The consensus of opinion seems to be there are three methods, depending on the time involved and the condition of the barrel (excessive fouling).

If a person has the time, brushing is not needed. Modern solvents will do an excellent job. They need some time to do that job. If there is no shooting the next day and you have the time to do the job correctly (make time), don't use a brush. You will reduce the odds of damage. Damage = loss of accuracy = money spent to re-crown or re-barrel. "Not brushing" is the first method and the safest.

If you are shooting a two-day match or Camp Perry, where you could be shooting a week or more day after day, you may want to use the "Patch-scrub method. "The solvents and abrasive cleaners are still doing the job but you are helping things along with some elbow grease. The odds of damage do go up so extra care is required.

I asked Charlie: "OK, so when should one use a brush in cleaning a barrel?" He said, "When there is evidence of excessive fouling in a barrel." "What evidence?" I ask. He replied "Look down the bore after firing a match; if you can see lines of copper, not just a slight copper color here and there, then you have excessive fouling. Brushing is required IF you don't have the time needed to let the solvent do the work."

The Tattle Tale and the Wooden Desk

I have three children, nine grandchildren, three Great-Grand kids, a brother, sisters, and assorted cousins. I KNOW what a tattletale is. Tattletales are seen as a life's negative, but they can come in handy when one of the other grand-babies is about to test her ability to fly from the third story window. The solvents: Hoppes, Sweets, and some others are tattletales. When they eat the copper deposits in the bore, they form a blue green sludge. The solvents are not only being a little tattletale about the copper still being in there, they are yelling, "Look at me, look at me." Anyone who is a parent will identify with that. The solvents are like any other tattletale; you're glad that they are telling you useful information, but you're annoyed (that the problem is still there) at the same time.

Charlie says "NEVER, NEVER, NEVER use a phosphor bronze brush (some people call them brass) with the stronger copper solvents. You can't know which is being eaten, the copper deposits or the bronze brush?"

Let's say you have an old wooden desk that needs to have the old paint removed. Lay a piece of sandpaper and a scrub brush on the desktop. No paint will be removed until you apply some motion or mechanical action. Oh, by the way, this is an expensive antique desk. Chucking up sandpaper or a brush in your power drill is not a good idea. A little elbow grease (for you people under age fifty, that's arm movement, applied with force, to accomplish a task) will do just fine.

Sandpaper (abrasive cleaners) and scrub brushing (bore brush) will do the job and will do it faster than the chemicals. The only concern is the extra care needed to prevent the accidental nick or ding. BT-Eliminator or Hoppes will slowly eat away at the copper and fouling and given time, will do a fine job.

Fig. 24
Bore Tech Eliminator

Note:
This is an update for this edition, Bore Tech Eliminator (Fig 24) is a bore cleaner and will do the job of cleaning the copper and fouling in five minutes verses the hours it

would take the Hoppes to do. With both cleaners you can leave it in the bore for a long period of time without harm and it will protect the metal as well.

These days, time is a precious commodity. Spiced with a little laziness, we want instant results (Dear God, give me patience and please give it to me NOW). Modern technology has taken us from, paint thinner to paint stripper (Sweets and the other great solvents). Pour some paint stripper on the desktop and the chemicals will start eating away faster. Given the time needed the chemicals must be removed. A scraper (dry patch) picks up and removes the loosened sludge created by the chemical reaction.

The solvents are full strength from the bottle. As they eat the fouling and copper deposits they lose their strength. The old sludge and weakened solvent has to be removed and a fresh coat of full strength solvent must be applied. With the stronger solvents you have to stay close at hand and remove them when the time is up. (BT-Eliminator or Hoppes) isn't as strong but you can run a wet patch through the bore and walk away for hours or days, without damage.

An Update

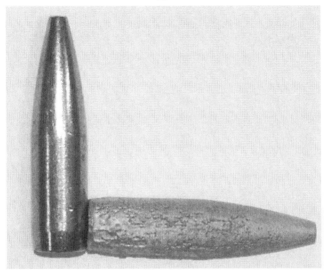

Fig. 25

This is a picture of a bullet (Fig. 25) that was soaked in KG 12 for twenty four hours. See the test results on my web site - products page
 http://www.jarheadtop.com/KG12_Test_Results.htm

There is no need to "Neutralize." KG 12 contains no ammonia. $9.95 a bottle plus $6.15 S&H (Priority Mail). My e-mail is Top@jarheadtop.com

Horror Stories

If the "National Foundation for Bad Examples" were to need a poster child, I could think of none more fitting than the common practice of barrel cleaning used in the late sixties. The shooter sat on his shooting stool with his M-14, muzzle up, held between his knees. Using a jointed metal rod and brush, he cleaned the barrel like he was churning butter. This boy not only holds up the one iron, he yells, "I dare you."

This next horror story was not a common practice, in fact it happened only once, but that was enough. The Marine Corps "Division" Matches are broken down into Teams. Each team member draws his or her shooting equipment and a rifle. After four to six weeks of shooting and the matches are over, the team must turn in all the equipment and the rifles. In the mad rush to clean the rifles, check out and the awards ceremony, things can get hectic.

The armorer knows if he accepts a rifle that is not clean, HE will have to clean it, so he is very careful to check the couple of thousand little places dirt and carbon can hide. One of the teams had a member with an ammo can of this "Wonder Cleaner" that would cut the dirt, carbon and time required all in one soaking. This wonder cleaner turned out to be "Freon." It did everything he said, but it also sucked out every last bit of oil or any other protection from the metal. All the team members passed inspection and were gone, but the next day every one of those rifles was solid RUST.

There is a modern version of this story going on today. Many Police Officers are cleaning their service revolvers with a wonderful product called "Birchwood-Casey Gun Scrubber." They spray down the pistol, shake off the excess and re holster. Fast, easy, time saving way to rust the firearm. The product is not bad, just the way it's used. You HAVE to re-oil and protect the metal, I recommend Bore Tech Gun Oil. Oh, by the way, Birchwood-Casey makes another great product to remove and prevent rust, it's called "Sheath."

Ground Rules for Cleaning the Barrel

Bolt rifles, M-14/M1A's, AR-15's and other types of rifles all have barrels. The ground rules for cleaning them are pretty much the same. The basic ground rules are: The direction to clean, protecting the crown, protecting the glass bedding, protecting the rifling, using the proper type rod, using a rod guide, using a cleaning rest, and using the products correctly. M1A's have a few extra considerations.

Care, Cleaning & Sportsmanship
The Direction to Clean

Bolt guns and AR-15's can have their bolts removed and you can clean them from the rear or breech end toward the front or muzzle. This is important because there is a lot of gunk, carbon residue, unspent powder and other nasty stuff in a barrel after a day of shooting. Particularly on the first pass, most of the large particles are removed. Pushing them out the muzzle where they can do no harm is the best solution. Pushing them into the chamber, glass bedding and trigger mechanism is asking for trouble.

The M1A MUST be placed in the cleaning rest **UPSIDE DOWN**. This does two things: 1) prevents the solvents from running into the passage way to the gas system, and 2) prevents the solvents from running into and destroying the glass bedding. AR-15's have no glass bedding so it's not important to clean them upside down. In fact, they should NOT be cleaned upside down, since their gas tube is on the top.

Fig. 26

UPDATE: This cleaning aid is designed for service rifles chambered in 243 Win, 308 Win, and 30-06 (M1, M1A, and M-14's). This receiver port inserts into your action and plugs the chamber just like a rod guide. Solvents are prevented from running down into the trigger group and into the bedding. It can also be used as an access port to apply more solvent prior to pulling your brush back through the bore. This receiver port also keeps the bolt in the open position and prevents you from ramming your brush or jag into the bolt face. (See Fig. 26 *Item 749-001-606WS - Sinclair Service Rifle Port*)

Special Note: This is a great product when used with a Non-Abrasive bore cleaner such as Hoppes. However if you are using an abrasive cleaner such as Remington Bore Cleaner or J.B. Bore cleaner **this cleaning aid will not protect the gas port** and the M1A should still be cleaned up-side down.

On the M-14/M1A, as the abrasive patch travels past the gas port, some of the abrasive (solids) will be wiped off the patch into the port. This will eventually deposit between the cylinder and piston right at the port and WILL cause galling of these surfaces which can effect accuracy and reliability. *THE GAS SYSTEM, INCLUDING PORT AND PASSAGE, MUST BE CLEANED BEFORE FIRING AFTER ABRASIVE CLEANERS HAVE BEEN USED.* A pipe cleaner can be used to clean the port and passage once the piston is removed; just be careful because the pipe cleaner has a wire inside it. The abrasive does not seem to affect the Ml or M16 in this manner.

Cleaning Rods

The proper size, coated, one piece rods such as a Dewey or Parker-Hale is "The Choice" of cleaning rods. Stay away from jointed or multi-sectional rods. Wood, fiber glass, aluminum or steel rods are harmful to the barrel. Wood or aluminum rods pick up and embed grit that later acts as a round sandpaper. Steel rods bang steel against steel causing dings.

Use a Rod Guide

The rod has to be supported at **BOTH ends**. The patch that touches all surfaces of the bore (or the brush) supports the rod as it travels down the bore. The rod guide supports and centers the rod as it starts down the barrel. The proper size rod and guide keeps the rod from flexing and banging into the rifling.

Charlie says a "cheap" rod guide for the M1A is to take a "used, empty" 12 gauge shot gun shell, drill out the primer pocket and slip the shell onto your cleaning rod. The shell fits nicely over the flash suppressor; centering and supporting the rod on its trip down the bore. There are a number of commercial rod guides available for the M1A.

For the bolt guns, Stoney Point has a couple of excellent rod guides. They have one that fits .17 to .25 cal., another fits .25 to .30 cal. and another that fits 8mm to .41 cal. The AR rifles have a nice rod guide in the "Dewey breech rod guide for M-16 and AR-15s." It has a "O" ring on the end that seals the bore so solvents cannot go where they are not wanted.

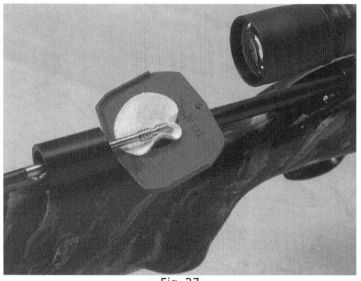

Fig. 27
This is a picture of a Bore Tech Rod Guide $59.95 + S&H

I carry this rod guide for the AR-15 and the patches for the AR-15. The guide fits into the chamber and has an O-Ring to seal the chamber. The patch is lays on the plate and is set off center to prevent a too tight a fit. The bore cleaner is then added to the patch and there is no chance of any cleaner entering the chamber or trigger group. For more information you can call me at 334-347-0020.

Jim Owens

Cleaning Rest

A portable cleaning rest is nice for all types of rifles, but on the M1A it is almost a must. Again, the upside down position keeps the solvents out of the gas system and the glass bedding. The MTM Case-gard RMC-1 Portable Maintenance Center for Rifles and Shotguns is a nice little tray and gun rest (see the source list).

If you ever want to learn a subject, try writing a book on it. Things we think we all know, and take for granted, really come "alive" when you try to give a logical reason for doing them. I had the startling realization that we all have a little of Tim Allen's macho in us when we clean our rifles after the match, talking to our friends. Bolt guns have glass bedding but we don't turn THEM upside down. Think about it. When we soak down that first patch to flush out the large particles of gunk in the bore we start the patch into the chamber. The chamber is about the size of the cartridge case, then it narrows to the neck size, then things narrow to the throat size and finally to the size of the bore. All this acts like a ringer on a mop bucket. It squeezes the excess liquid and leaves it in the chamber area. I don't care how much you promised your mother you won't let gravity take the solvent down into the glass bedding; it's going there. SO, promise your mother you will use a bore guide that seals.

Special Precautions for the M1A

The bolt stop is spring loaded. When the magazine is removed the bolt stop still holds the bolt open. When the op-rod is pulled back a little, the spring on the bolt stop moves it out of the way and the bolt can be closed. It's a fine system.

There is a fine line between looking like a professional and looking like a klutz. Pushing a cleaning rod down a bore with a tight patch requires some force. Trouble is, when the patch reaches the chamber area, the force is no longer required. You may have been pushing hard and suddenly the rod flies forward, slamming into the face of the bolt, pushing it back.

Care, Cleaning & Sportsmanship

The bolt stop moves out of the way, releasing the bolt. Now the op-rod spring takes the op-rod and the bolt and slams them into your patch holder and cleaning rod. Unless you already have a reputation as a klutz, it is something you may want to avoid.

Just forward of the rear sight is a slot called the charger guide; the charger guide is used for a rapid reload of the M-14 magazine. The mag. is placed in the rifle and a stripper clip full of rounds is placed in the charger guide. Pushing down on the rounds loads them into the mag. while the charger guide keeps everything aligned.

Take an empty stripper clip and place it into the charger guide, pull back on the op-rod to release the bolt stop and let the bolt slide forward until it touches the stripper clip. The bolt cannot slam into brushes, patch holders, cleaning rods or fingers. A simple stripper clip can make you look like a professional.

While you're at it, make sure your rear sight is all the way down. It should already be down because you are a professional and you counted down your elevation to confirm that your sights aren't running and to record your zero in your data book. Leaving the sight raised during cleaning can cause expensive damage. Again, another fine line.

Jim Owens

What is the Fundamental, Always Works Cleaning Routine?

That is one of the questions asked by a reader. Well, here goes. This is the Charlie Milazzo, fundamental, always works, will not harm the barrel or other major parts, cleaning method. We are going to use the M1A because it requires a few extra considerations (most have been covered in detail earlier).

You have just finished your last string of fire and the barrel is hot. You have to either keep score or go to the pits next or proceed to the Wailing Wall for the whining hour. Keeping in mind the ground rules: Type of rod, using a rod guide, clean upside down, placing a stripper clip in the charging guide and running the sights down. You want to run a wet patch soaked with BT-Eliminator or Hoppes down the bore (while it's hot) to flush out the large particles and to let the solvent start to loosen the grime.

Remember, the first loose fitting wet patch only is from the muzzle end to avoid running the rod over any grit in the bore. You want to clean from the breech (chamber) to the muzzle (less chance to damage the crown). Guide the rod past the flash suppressor (muzzle) and past the crown. Slip the rod guide into place and push the rod down the bore until it exits the chamber. Place a loose patch soaked with BT-Eliminator or Hoppes on a slotted, aluminum or plastic patch holder. The patch should touch all surfaces of the bore but should not be so tight it would require a lot of force to push or pull the rod down the barrel. Screw on the patch holder and patch in the mag. well. **<u>Caution: twist the patch holder and NOT THE ROD</u>**. You don't want the rod to embed any grit into the coating. Now PULL the rod through the bore to flush out the large particles. One pass is all that's needed. Remove the patch and wipe the rod clean to prevent any particles from embedding into the coating.

Remove the stripper clip and let the bolt go home on a dry

Care, Cleaning & Sportsmanship

patch to seal the chamber area and prevent solvent from running down into the bedding. Wrap a paper towel around the flash suppressor and place a large plastic sandwich bag over the flash suppressor and place the rifle in your gun case. Now head on down to the pits or keep score. Remember the solvent needs the time to work.

When you come out of the pits and are waiting for the stat office to post the scores on the Wailing Wall, you can give the barrel another swipe. Remove the sandwich bag and paper towel. Remove the dry patch when you open the bolt. Reinsert the stripper clip in the charging guide and release the bolt onto the clip. Again upside down, carefully feed the rod (without the patch holder) down the barrel. Screw on the patch holder and a dry patch in the mag well. Now pull the rod and the dry patch down the bore to take up the loosened gunk. Repeat with a fresh patch. Two or three dry patches are fine, then _REPEAT WITH A WET PATCH_. Repeat the procedures for transport: dry patch on the closed bolt, paper towel and sandwich bag to protect the gun case. Put the rifle away and you're ready to go home.

You can repeat the above procedure when you get home before you clean up and have dinner. A few hours later, after the solvent has had time to work, you can again run a few dry patches. Now that you're home and without the distractions of a lot of people talking, you may want to get a little more aggressive. In this first method, aggressive means a more powerful solvent, not elbow grease.

A good solvent to use here is Sweet's 7.62 Solvent. Again, with the rifle upside down and the stripper clip in place, run a loose patch soaked with the Sweets in the bore (Boots says to leave the Sweets in the bore at least 10 min. but no more than 15 min.) At the end of the 10 - 15 min. time, run a dry patch through the bore and look for the blue green tattle tale color, proof the solvent is eating the copper deposits.

Repeat the dry patch a couple of times then repeat the wet patch with the Sweets. Again, let stand 10 - 15 min. and dry patch a few times. The tattletale will let you know how things are going. You can usually do two, three, or four passes with the more powerful solvent and it will be sufficient. Charlie, Boots, Jack, and Mike all say that the problems occur when you try to over-clean the barrel.

Keep in mind you're not going to get out every last bit of copper and you don't need too. **Wrap up your Sweets cleaning by running a wet patch with BT-Eliminator or Hoppes through to neutralize the more powerful cleaner (Sweets or any other solvent you choose)**. Leave the wet BT-Eliminator or Hoppes in the bore to protect it from humidity and it will continue to attack any remaining copper. Be sure to use the dry patch on the closed bolt and store the rifle muzzle down. Charlie says that resting the rifle on the flash suppressor will not hurt it, just do it gently. If you are concerned about standing the rifle on the flash suppressor, you can hang the rifle from the butt swivel. If it falls from the hanger it WON'T land gently!

Do you want a real surprise? Take a barrel you think is clean and run a wet patch with BT-Eliminator or Hoppes down the bore and let it stand from 24 to 48 hours. The BT-Eliminator or Hoppes will not harm the barrel and will protect it from humidity. NEVER store a bore dry. At the end of the 24 to 48 hours run a dry patch through the barrel. The tattletale blue green will surprise you. The 24 to 48 hours has given the BT-Eliminator or Hoppes the time it needs to do a really good job.

The next time you get to the range, don't just pull the rifle out of the case and start firing. The bullet will have to travel through a lot of blue green sludge and will be nowhere near where your sighters should be. When you take the rifle out of the case, run several dry patches down the bore to remove the NEW loosened sludge. **As a last step before firing you may want to run a patch with lighter fluid down the bore to make sure it is perfectly dry.**

Boots' Favorite

Boots has a favorite bore cleaner. It used to be called "*Gold Medallion.*" They changed the name to "*Remclean.*" Mike told me they changed the name again to "*Remington Bore Cleaner.*" By the time you read this, who knows what they will be calling it? It's an abrasive cleaner and gets the job done "lickity split" (Again, for you folks under age 50 that means fast.) **Warning**: special precautions are required with abrasive bore cleaners. Another more abrasive cleaner is JB Bore Cleaner. Clint Fowler said that after 500 or so rounds, a cleaning with JB bore cleaner does wonders.

The abrasive cleaners contain sandpaper grit required to remove the fouling. They require the elbow grease movement. Just running them through and letting them sit doesn't get the job done. A scrubbing action is required. Potential damage to the crown is the main consideration. However, not removing all of the leftover abrasive grit can cause its own problems.

Let's use a little common sense concerning abrasive cleaners. *Remclean* is a liquid with mild abrasives suspended in the cleaner. Scrubbing the bore with a dry patch isn't going to cut the mustard; you need the abrasive grit. A liberal amount is required to coat the patch on all surfaces. Remember our mop ringer: the chamber area narrowing to the neck size, then to the throat, and finally, narrowing to the bore size. The excess liquid is going to be squeezed out and will remain in the chamber and throat area. If you don't flush out the grit, the cartridge case (in the chamber) and the bullet (in the throat and bore) will pick up the abrasive. Round after round of this will cause wear on parts you don't want.

JB Bore Cleaner is a paste of stronger abrasive. A barrel that's starting to lose its accuracy may benefit from a scrubbing with JB Bore Cleaner. Where the chamber meets the throat area is a tiny lip or ledge. The abrasive cleaner tends to build up at the six o'clock position on that ledge. Again, if you don't flush out the grit, the bullet will pick up the grit and cause wear on the rifling.

Jim Owens

How tight is Tight?

The terms loose patch and tight patch are relative terms. It's like cold and hot; there are varying degrees (pun intended).

You want a loose patch to flush the large particles after shooting and to flush the abrasive cleaners after scrubbing the bore. The best way to get a loose patch is to use a slotted tip. Take a square patch and fold the opposite corners together to form a triangle. If you place one end of the patch just a little into the slot, the patch will pull free as it's placed in the rifle. The more you pull the patch into the slot, the tighter the patch will be (up to half way). <u>Pulling the patch about one third of the way through the slot will usually be sufficient to allow the patch to touch all the surfaces of the bore while not requiring any great amount of force to push the rod through the barrel.</u>

To clean out the loosened fouling or to scrub the bore with abrasive cleaners, a tight patch is required. How tight is tight? I've seen patches so loose they fall off the holder when placed in the rifle. Others slide through the bore with little or no resistance. A patch that requires a <u>moderate amount of force</u> is the correct "tight patch." When the patch is so tight you have to use a lot of force to push it down the bore, it's too tight. When the rod flexes, the patch is too tight. Sometimes the shooter next to you has a patch so tight you can hear it squeak as it travels down the barrel. The next one he really wraps tight and asks you to pull on the rod while he pulls on the rifle to release the stuck patch.

For a loose patch, the slotted tip works best. For a tight patch the "European-Style Jag" is the one to use. Charlie likes the Parker-Hale Jag but he does not care for the Dewey Jag. Some of the jags have a sharp point on the end. Stabbing a patch in the center and running it down the bore will have you in a game of tug of war with someone to free it from the barrel. On the "European-Style Jag" an adapter is required because both the cleaning rod and the jag have external or male threads. The adapter has internal or female threads on both ends. Champions Choice, Creedmoor and most all the other shooting supply stores carry them (most rods come with them).

The patch being too tight can be caused by several factors. The patch just may be too large. A sharp knife or scissors will cut the patch down enough to give it a snug fit. Sometimes the patch needs to be cut in half or maybe just removing a third is sufficient. The main reason for too tight of a patch is the angle the patch is fed onto the jag. One angle will make the patch long and skinny while another angle will make it short and fat. Trial and error plus experience will determine what works for you.

Note: I carry the 1 1/8th patches needed for the AR-15. Do not put the point of the jag in the center of the patch, which will make it too tight in the bore. Offset the jag. On the 1st pass offset it high and on the next pass offset it low. This will give full coverage to the bore without being too tight.

The Two Step Scrub Method

You have just finished today's match and you have to shoot again tomorrow; your barrel is hot and you want to do a cleaning now and not have to think about it again until tomorrow.

Again, remember the usual ground rules and precautions: proper rod, rod guide, stripper clip to hold the bolt open, cleaning rest, rifle upside down to protect the gas system and glass bedding.

First, flush out the large particles with a loose patch soaked in BT-Eliminator or Hoppes. If you have to rush down to the pits or keep score you can leave the rifle in the rest or place it in the gun case; remember to close the bolt on a dry patch and protect the case with a dry paper towel and sandwich bag. If you don't have to rush off immediately, you can finish the job while the barrel is still hot.

After the rod has made the first pass with the loose patch soaked with BT-Eliminator or Hoppes to flush out the large particles, unscrew the slotted tip and remove the patch. Pull the rod back out of the bore and wipe the rod with a clean rag. Now place the adapter and the jag on the rod. With a patch cut to the proper size, rotate it around the jag. Remember you want a tight (snug) patch, not one that squeaks (over tight) as it goes through the bore.

Make sure you shake the bottle of Remclean before using. The abrasive particles tend to settle; they should be suspended in the liquid. Apply a liberal amount to the patch. Feed the patch from the chamber end (the shape of the chamber acts as a natural funnel to gradually compress the patch, which focuses the pressure in the most important area — the throat). Start a scrubbing motion down the bore, two inches forward and one inch back. Remove the rod from the muzzle end. Wipe the rod with a clean patch and repeat the scrubbing on the next pass.

If you're cleaning a bolt gun or AR-15 from the breech, be careful when you get to the muzzle and crown. **Do not exit the patch by more than one half of an inch. If you do exit, DO NOT pull the patch back into the bore, remove it.** The abrasive cleaner will wear on the crown when the patch re-compresses. Remove the patch and carefully feed the jag and adapter past the crown. Remove the rod, wipe it with a clean patch and repeat the scrubbing on the next pass.

I asked: "How many times should one scrub the bore with the abrasive cleaners?" Mike says that you can "feel" when the job is done. The first pass will feel rough; the second pass should feel smooth, so the third pass will also feel smooth. Charlie sarcastically says, "Anything worth doing, is worth overdoing (If some is good, and more is better, then too much should be just about right)." "If you do the fourth pass, you're becoming an anal retentive." Thirty years ago I asked pretty much the same question at the Eastern Division Matches. The Instructor said "Ten passes for each shot fired." Hmmmm, sixty rounds a day times ten, now that's anal-retentive!

M-14 Caution

Repeated from earlier

On the M-14/M1A, as the abrasive patch travels past the gas port, some of the abrasive (solids) will be wiped off the patch into the port. This will eventually deposit between the cylinder and piston right at the port and WILL cause galling of these surfaces which can effect accuracy and reliability. <u>THE GAS SYSTEM, INCLUDING PORT AND PASSAGE, MUST BE CLEANED BEFORE FIRING AFTER ABRASIVE CLEANERS HAVE BEEN USED.</u> A pipe cleaner can be used to clean the port and passage once the piston is removed; just be careful because the pipe cleaner has a wire inside it. The abrasive does not seem to affect the Ml or M16 in this manner.

Be sure to use a fresh patch and new cleaner on each pass. Now wipe down the rod with a clean rag and change the tip back to the slotted one. With a loose patch soaked in BT-Eliminator or Hoppes, flush out the abrasive grit a time or two. Leave the barrel wet and the BT-Eliminator or Hoppes will continue to clean and protect the bore.

Remember, the next day as soon as you remove the rifle from the case and make it safe (cleared), run a dry patch or two down the bore to remove any loosened copper fouling the Hoppes ate overnight.

Get a Rope

If you have ever lived in a barracks, you will have learned something about scrubbing. Every Friday is "Barracks Inspection." Every Thursday night is "Field Day;" the barracks is cleaned and scrubbed from top to bottom. Particularly interesting is when the platoon of Marines has come in from the field at 0100 (1:00 AM) with muddy boots. The mud has dried and the floor is caked in dirt.

The dirt has to be loosened by scrubbing, then it is mopped away. Using a dry scrub brush will not do the job. The floor must be wet and a hard scrubbing action is required. Once the dirt is broken up and loosened, it requires frequent passes with a clean mop to lift the dirt from the floor.

Oh, by the way, if you ever do have to live in a barracks, a word of caution: the concrete floor is a dull, dingy, gray color. If you are assigned a "Cube" or cubical (formed by wall lockers) each person is assigned to clean their own space.

DON'T use Tide laundry detergent to scrub your cube. That one white square area stands out like the proverbial sore thumb. You will be running for the hills, while the rest of the barracks yells, "Get a Rope!"

Brushing

Let's clear up a little confusion. Some people think you should never use a bronze or brass brush. The truth is: Brass Core, Phosphor-Bronze Brushes are great, IF you use them with the proper liquid, like Hoppes or the abrasive cleaners. The problem occurs when you use the stronger solvents like Sweets or some of the others. Soak a patch with Sweets and wrap it around a Brass Core, Phosphor-Bronze Brush and watch the blue-green appear. The tattletale can't tell the truth if it's eating the brush instead of the copper fouling.

Nylon brushes are OK if you use the abrasive cleaners, but aren't much use with just Hoppes as they are too wimpy (tech term). Don't use a stainless steel brush; you don't need a brush on steroids.

For you youngsters (under age fifty) who can remember the child's game "Pickup Sticks," and for the rest of you, picture a small twig. One stick by itself can be easily broken. A bundle of sticks or twigs has greater resistance when it comes to trying to break them. An individual bronze wire would be easily bent and broken. When hundreds of these little wires are bundled together in a rotary pattern, you have a stiff and strong wire brush.

Getting the Right Size

Obviously, running a .22 cal. brush down a .30 cal. barrel isn't going to work because the bristles will not touch all the sides of the bore. If you could make it fit, a .45 cal. brush down a .30 cal. barrel would have the bristles lay over so far there wouldn't be any contact of the bristle tips to the bore.

"Well, nit wit," you say, "Use a .30 cal. brush in a .30 cal. barrel." Of course you're right . . . to a point. A NEW .30 cal. brush is a little too large to do an effective scrubbing action. "Explain yourself, McDuff.'

When a new .30 cal. brush starts down a .30 cal. barrel the bristles bend back. They bend at the core of the brush and remain straight. The tips will make contact on the bore and will scrub as they travel the length of the bore. Reversing the direction of travel while in the bore (if you can) will cause damage to the new brush. The bristles are in a tight fit and they cannot reverse direction without bending—a lot. It's like a slat in a Venetian blind; it will bend and snap back rather easily, but bend it too much and a crease will occur. It will never bounce back.

A used brush that has worn down a little is best for the scrubbing action. I told Charlie, "This is like the situation of you can't get the job unless you have experience and you can't get experience unless you have the job." So, give your new brushes a part-time job.

Brushing to clean a barrel is an occasional method, such as excessive fouling or between stages of a match. **<u>The chemical or the patch scrub method is by far preferred for routine cleaning</u>**. From time to time, with the first two methods, run a new brush down the barrel. Always run it in one direction only and exit the bore completely. This applies anytime you use a brush.

Charlie said some guy wrote an article saying brushing should always be from the muzzle to the breech, to protect the throat. He highly disagrees. For one thing, the bristles act as a miniature catapult, hurling the crud into the chamber, trigger, and the bedding. More important, damage to the crown is easier to do and far more serious. Once the bullet leaves the crown, there is nothing to overcome or re-stabilize it if there are any nicks or defects. The damage is done.

A brush that is well worn and too loose will slide over the rifling and will cause wear patterns you don't want. How do you tell if it's too loose? Hold the rifle vertically and with the brush on the rod place it carefully past the crown. If the rod moves by its own weight, the brush is too loose and should be replaced.

How do you tell when the brush is the right size for scrubbing? Charlie says it's an "Acquired Feel." It will not have the same resistance or force required with a new brush. Until you get the Acquired Feel you may ruin a few new brushes, but brushes are a lot cheaper than barrels.

A "Commandment"

Here is a commandment from Moses himself (OK, Charlie only LOOKS like Moses). **"ALWAYS" use a loose patch wrapped around the brush when brushing the barrel**. This applies to new, old, used, brass, bronze or nylon brushes. Two reasons: 1) the patch holds more solvent close to the tip of the bristles where it's needed and 2) the patch picks up the loosened crud and carries it away.

You think the bristles can't get through the patch to scrub the bore? Wrap a patch around a brush and squeeze hard with two fingers; it *will* bite you.

Fig. 28
Otis- M-16 Chamber Brush

Designed to clean the chamber and lug recess area. The front brush has bronze bristles with a stainless steel core while the rear portion has longer stainless steel bristles. Brush is male threaded 8-32.

All the other precautions and steps are the same with the brush scrub method as the patch scrub method. Remember to use extra care to flush the grit and crud from the bore, and *CLEAN THE CHAMBER!!*

Fig. 29

This one of a kind tool (Fig 29) is used to clean the lug recess area on the AR-15 and AR-10 rifles. The lug recess area collects a lot of grease and debris and needs to be cleaned regularly. This tool compresses a cotton roll and then releases it so you can rotate it inside the lug recess area. Should be used wet with solvent, then followed up with a dry roll. One bag of cotton rolls, about 50, is included with each tool.

749-003-995WS
Sinclair AR-15 Lug Recess Tool with Rolls

Fig. 30

This item is a must have for cleaning your AR-15. The Link separates the upper and lower assemblies (Fig 30), but holds them securely to allow easy breech access for bore cleaning using a Sinclair Rod Guide. Made of Delrin and stainless steel, it is virtually impervious to solvents. The Cleaning Link uses the rear locking pin and rear locking pin hole and installs in seconds

749-002-497WS
Sinclair AR-15 Cleaning Link

CHAPTER THREE

Cleaning the AR-15

THE CARE AND FEEDING OF YOUR AR STYLE RIFLE
by
Myles Gorin - Coach, Arizona Rifle Team

A happy rifle is one that is clean and well lubricated. To accomplish this, you have to start with the proper equipment. It's not worth buying "cheap". Cleaning Rod- needs to be a solid, plastic coated rod. Uncoated rods can scratch the bore, and the microscopic height differences in screw together rod sections can cause chipping on the crown and scratches in the bore. Bore Guide- a Nylon unit that firmly seats into the chamber is essential.

You need to push the patches through the barrel in the same direction as bullet flight. Only exception to pulling something backwards is the scrubbing brush. **Jag** screwed onto the end of the rod, it is used to push quality cotton patches through the bore. This is superior to putting the patch onto a loop. **Bore Brush**-screwed onto the end of the rod, it is used to dislodge carbon fouling in the bore. A good quality Nylon brush is preferred. **Chamber Brush**- Wrap a shotgun patch around the brush, and you have an effective way of wiping out the chamber. **Solvents**- There are many excellent firearms cleaning products on the market, and all come with their manufacturer's recommended procedures.

The products and techniques described herein are proven to be effective, but are no means expected to be gospel. Utilize what works. First, never use water displacing lubricants such as WD-40 on you gun. It will render your primers inert. The best "good old standby" is Hoppes No.9. I use this last as a neutralizer. Bore Tech Eliminator is fantastic for removing carbon and light copper deposits. For heavy carbon fouling, Slip 2000's Carbon Cutter is the ticket. For heavy copper fouling, Bore Tech Cu+2 Copper Remover will take out the worst copper build up.

The Bore Tech, Hoppe's and Slip 2000 products mentioned here do not contain ammonia and may be left in the barrel for extended periods of soaking. **Other copper removers such as Sweet's 7.62, Montana X-treme and KG Bore Cleaner are labeled to NOT remain in the barrel for extended periods of time.** Slip 2000's 725 degreaser works as advertised. It is water-soluble however, and will cause rust on steel if not removed. Wear rubber gloves and eye protection when handling the solvents. **Lubrication**- Slip 2000's EWL or other oil is used to lubricate moving parts, especially the bolt. You do not want to operate a bolt dry. Apply a light coating of grease to the bolt carrier friction points. Needle Nose Pliers- used in dissembling the bolt assembly.

Carbon scraper- used to remove carbon build-up inside the bolt carrier. Dental pick- Very useful tool for small parts. Q-tips with long sticks. How often you need to clean your rifle depends on numerous considerations. You should normally plan on disassembly and cleaning every 200 rounds or so. However, if you have a wet or dusty day at the range, you will want to clean after the outing. Water left in the gun will cause rust, and sand & dust will result in premature wearing of metal parts.

Between shooting sessions where you will not be cleaning the rifle, it would be a good idea to push a couple of dry patches through the bore, wipe the chamber and area behind the locking lugs with a chamber brush wrapped with a shotgun patch, and lubricate the bolt.

It must also be pointed out that you do not want to go into an important match with a perfectly clean bore. Bullet trajectory on a perfectly clean bore will be different than expected. Fouling shots must be done prior to first shots of record.

Last item is proper new barrel break-in. It is essential to barrel life and accuracy. New barrels have the bore and chambers polished smooth during the manufacturing process, but cutting oils and chips can be left behind. The one area that does not have a perfect surface is the throat, the transition area between the chamber and the barrel bore. This area gets smoothed out from fire lapping, the interaction of the fired bullet and the surface. What happens is the copper jacket of the bullets interacts with the rough surface of the throat, and some copper from the bullet jacket turns to plasma which settles inside the bore. As this copper builds in the bore, if deforms the bullets as they pass through, effecting the flight dynamics of the bullet. A proper break-in cleaning session prevents the copper build-up.

All barrel manufacturers post some regiment of break-in on their websites. Generally proper break-in is a thorough cleaning of the new bore, followed by 10 cycles of shooting one shot and cleaning, then 5 cycles of shooting two shots and cleaning, and finely, 2 cycles of shooting five shots and cleaning. This is a total of 30 shots.

The Cleaning

First VERIFY that the rifle is EMPTY. Too many "empty" guns have been involved with blown out TV's.

"Break" the rifle in half. Starting with the upper or lower is your choice.

Lower- Spray 725 Degreaser in the trigger housing. Swish with a Q-tip. Repeat if necessary. Blow out debris and solvent with air gun. Place a drop of gun oil (EWL) on the trigger springs, and grease on the sear contact points. If it's been a while, remove the buffer and spring from the tube. After cleaning, place a light coating of grease on the spring before re-inserting.

Upper- Remove the bolt carrier and charging handle and set aside. Spray the inside of the receiver and behind the locking lugs with 725 Degreaser, and swish with a Q-tip. Blow out debris and solvent with air gun. Flush the gas tube with break cleaner.

Insert the bore guide into the chamber. Push several patches wet with Bore Tech Eliminator through the bore with the jag on the rod. Put the Nylon brush onto the rod, wet the brush with Bore Tech, and run it completely in then out of the bore 15 to 20 times. Never reverse direction of the brush while inside the bore.

Put the jag back onto the rod and push through several more patches wet with Bore Tech. Now push through a number of dry patches to sop up most of the Bore Tech and debris. Next step, several patches wet with Hoppe's No. 9 Solvent. This will "neutralize" the Bore Tech and give you that good "clean gun" smell. Almost all evidence of carbon and copper should be gone. Use several dry patches to sop up the Hoppe's.

If you are lucky enough to have access to a bore scope, you can get an up close look at the bore to see how good of a job you did.

If there is excessive carbon fouling, follow the wet patch / brushing routine using Slip 2000 Carbon Killer. For excessive copper buildup, do the same routine using Bore Tech's Cu+2 Copper Remover.

If heavier cleaning is required to remove fouling, several patches with J-B Compound may be passed through the bore. Push with a scrubbing action, 2 or 3 inches forward and 1 or 2 inches backward. Do not pull a patch back past the crown, as excessive wear will occur. Repeat the above steps to remove the J-B Compound and the residue it loosened. Then flush the gun extremely well with patches wet with Hoppe's No. 9 to remove all of the J-B mild abrasive grit.

If the gun is going to be stored for a while, push through a couple of patches wet with gun oil, followed by a couple of dry patches to sop up the excess oil.

Remove the bore guide, and wipe out the chamber with a brush wrapped with a shot gun patch.

Bolt and Carrier- Remove the firing pin, pull the bolt out of the carrier, and remove the extractor from the bolt. Clean all with 725 Degreaser. Use a toothbrush on stubborn spots. Blow dry with the air gun.

Use the carbon scraper on the bolt end and inside the bolt carrier.

Place a touch of grease inside the extractor contact area on the bolt. Install the extractor and replace the retaining pin. Verify that the gap in the three gas rings do not line up. Wet the bolt with oil (EWL).

Wet the inside of the bolt with oil (EWL). Slide the bolt into the carrier, replace the cam pin and firing pin, and insert the cotter pin.

Lightly place grease on the bolt carrier contact areas, wipe the carrier with oil (EWL), and force oil into the two oil holes.

Replace the charging handle in the upper, and seat the bolt into barrier. Re-assemble the upper and lower rifle halves.

Dry-fire function test the rifle, and you are ready to go.
Used with permission, M.D. Gorin Coach, Arizona Rifle Team ©2015

M-14/M1A Gas System

I love magic! David Copperfield is the King of magic. I can't wait until he has a new special. In the meantime, I saw a TV show with many magic acts. The lead act had a Bengal Tiger in a fiberglass cage being lifted about twenty feet above the stage. A loud noise, a big puff of smoke, and the cage falls apart, hanging vertically.

In a flash, my mind thinks that kitty will land on his feet, but when he does, he's going to have an attitude and maybe have a serious talk with his stage partner. The smoke instantly clears and the tiger is in another cage, on the left side of the stage. Now, two things come to mind: a) that cat didn't have time to fall straight down, much less diagonally across the stage and b) even if he did that's one smart cat. I love magic!

On that same TV show they had a magician who showed a "small" magic trick just before the commercials and then showed how he did it just after the commercials. I know the magician's assistant is supposed to distract you and it must work; because of Winona Ryder's low cut dress, I still cannot remember how he did most of the tricks.

Marine Corps Magic

I've been retired from the Marine Corps over twenty five years now. Since the statute of limitations has expired, I'm going to pass along a bit of the Marine Corps Team's magic. Charlie won't wear the low cut dress. (Furry Cleavage?)

On Marine Corps Base, Quantico, Va., range four, at the little end of the three hundred-yard line, sits a small white building known as "The Test Shed." Tommy Riddle was one of the best coaches the Marine Corps Team ever had. When he retired in 1983 he took over running the test shed. He invited me in one afternoon. I got to go behind the curtain with the Wizard of Oz.

The test shed could hold two people comfortably. Along one wall was a rifle rack filled with M-14's, fresh from the RTE shop (Rifle Team Equipment, where the real David Copperfield's disguised as gunsmiths did their magic). The Wizard's operation was quite simple. He would place an M-14 in the rifle rest and radio the Pvt. in the pits to run up the target. He then would fire a five round group (I think it was five rounds, sometimes I mis-remember). The Pvt. would pull the target and measure the group. The rifle had to shoot a group no larger than 2-1/2" wide by 1-1/2" high at three hundred yards (the X-ring is 3" in diameter). If the group was too large, they would make an adjustment (the magic) and do it again, and again, and again, and again until they got the proper group size.

The Real Secret

The members of the summer team never knew the secret that allowed them to have some fantastic shooting rifles. If the Pvt. called back with too large a group size, Tommy would simply unscrew the gas cylinder plug and remove the gas piston. He would reach up to a shelf that held row on row of gas pistons and picks another one. He placed it in the rifle, screwed down the gas cylinder plug to the proper torque and fired another group, repeating the process again and again, until he had the desired group size. The rifle was then placed in the other rack, ready for issue.

As interesting as that may be, the average civilian doesn't have a test shed with row on row of gas pistons. As wonderful as magic is, it has a debilitating *effect*: it makes the magician look like a God or Wizard, and we feel there is nothing we can do that compares. It's just not true! Once we take away the mysticism and show you a few simple procedures, you will be closer to the "Gods."

The More I Learn, the Less I Know

Jack Krieger says, "The more I learn, the more I wonder how I was able to hit anything." We all agree.

My Grandchildren already think I'm older than dirt. I'm starting to agree. Back in the mid-1960s I was in the dark ages of gun care. I look back on our procedures and I believe I went Distinguished not because of my care and cleaning techniques, but in spite of them.

During an important team match I went back to the 600-yard line down only one point. Part way through the string my shots started to go all over the target. I thought: "Oh God, not now." I heard a teammate call my name and when I looked back, he held up a bottle of Hoppes. Sure enough, my gas piston was stuck. In those days you poured a few drops in the vent hole to keep the piston loose. I now know it works, FOR A VERY SHORT TIME. It only makes matters worse later. Our only saving grace was having an armory full of M-14's that we could screw up, <u>one at a time</u>.

Let's Look Inside

Our imaginary ant has to go around an open manhole on his trip down the "tunnel." There is a hole or passageway for the gases at the six o'clock position of the bore. It passes an open "Door" and into a gas chamber. The gas cylinder is a reservoir for the gases. The gas piston has a small range of travel and MUST be free to move.

When you squeeze the trigger, the hammer falls, strikes the firing pin, and slams it into the primer, causing an explosion in the cartridge, and hurling the bullet and gases down the bore. Some of the gases take the passage into the gas system. They hit the gas piston like a croquet mallet hitting the wooden ball, transferring the energy to the op-rod. The op-rod slides through the op-rod guide and compresses the op-rod spring. On the other end the op-rod slides to the rear in the receiver tracks. The bolt roller is set in the op-rod recess and takes the bolt to the rear along with the op-rod.

The bolt grabs the empty case and "extracts" it from the chamber. It then ejects it from the rifle into a) your stool, b) into tall grass, c) down gopher holes, d) other places you can't find, or e) if you're real lucky, down the neck of your opponent to the right. At the same time the bolt is cocking the hammer for the next shot. Then, the op-rod spring expands, taking the op-rod, the bolt roller, and the bolt forward. The bolt strips a round out of the magazine and pushes it into the chamber for the next shot.

Start a Few Good Habits

"Dirty Dave" Yinglig was a prankster. He pulled the bullet and emptied the powder from the case. With the live primer and powder residue he chambered the empty case and closed the bolt on the M-14, waiting for the armorer to come by. He told the armorer, "This trigger doesn't feel right, would you check it?" The poor sap didn't check to see if the rifle was safe; he pulled the trigger. He jumped a foot when there was a loud POP and flame came out of the muzzle. From that day on, I trusted NO ONE. When I pick up a rifle I check to see if the chamber is empty. Even if you hand it to your best friend, when that rifle returns to your hands, CHECK IT!!!

Testing for Accuracy

People who know about this little "test" only perform it when they happen to remember it. This test is to accuracy, as checking the chamber is to safety. EVERY TIME YOU PICK UP AN M-14/M1A

1) Check the chamber, and 2) perform this little test. With the bolt open, hold the rifle at about a forty-five degree angle, muzzle up, to the two o'clock position. Listen carefully, as you rotate the muzzle to about a forty-five degree angle down, five o'clock position. The piston should slide in the gas system, and you can hear it. It will make a distinctive sound as it bottoms out. Then return the muzzle to about a forty-five degree angle up. Again you should hear the piston slide and it will make a different distinctive sound. Repeat it several times.

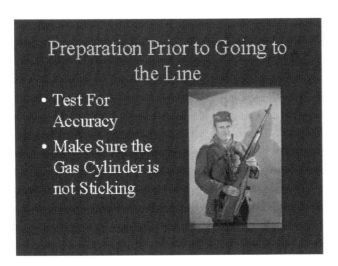

Fig. 31

In Fig 31, the rifle is angled up.

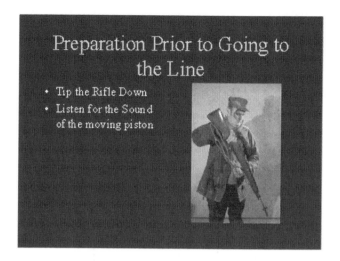

Fig. 32

In Fig 32, the rifle is angled down.

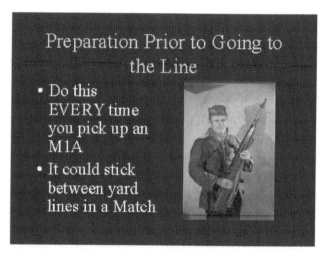

Fig. 33

In Fig 33, the rifle is angled up again.

You may have checked it in the morning, but halfway through the match the piston can freeze up. If you get into the habit of checking it <u>every time you pick up the rifle</u>, you will be accomplishing several things: a) you will know it is currently OK, b) you will get familiar with the speed of movement and

Care, Cleaning & Sportsmanship

the sounds of the piston and c) you will detect impending problems due to carbon build up and reduced piston speed.

How Often to Break Down and Clean?

I asked Charlie that question and he gave me the typical technocrat's answer: "There are so many variables: the primer & powder combination has a lot to do with how dirty a load is, the lubricants used, the amount of humidity in your area, the phases of the moon, etc. etc."

OK Charlie, how can the average Joe Blow tell when to break down the gas system and clean it? "If you are looking for a number, I'll pull one out of the air and say at least every 500 rounds. But more important it's like taking the receiver out of the bedding: AS NEEDED." Yes, the end of the shooting season is one of the needed times to check for problems, and a tune-up. Other needed times are when problems occur. The best way to know when there is a problem is to keep a log; even your score book will do. Record the information and when you see your group sizes enlarge and you see no other reason, this could be an "as needed" time. It could come in 480 rounds or 360 rounds; the log will tell you if you tell it the info it needs. Your best indicator is the "tilt" test, listen to the sound and keep track of the movement rate.

What Causes the Problem?

The piston itself is hollow on one end and the gas cylinder plug is also hollow. Together they form the gas reservoir. When the gases are pushing the bullet down the bore, some of the gases take the connecting passage to the gas system and into the reservoir. As the reservoir is filling, the bullet is still being pushed down the bore. If the system is clean and everything is working as advertised, right after the bullet leaves the muzzle, the gases will have filled the reservoir enough to start moving the gas piston, which immediately cuts off the passage so no more gas can enter the system. The system has the exact amount of gas needed to do the job. Too little and the system will not function properly (short cycling, failure to extract, failure to eject). Too much gas and damage could occur to the op-rod and other parts.

The problem comes when carbon builds. Every time the rifle fires and gases enter the gas system, carbon is built up on the walls of the reservoir, both on the gas cylinder plug and inside the piston itself. The carbon clings to the walls, and shot after shot builds layer on layer. Eventually the interior size of the reservoir is reduced in volume to the point where the gases fill the chamber sooner and the op-rod starts to move BEFORE the bullet has had a chance to exit the muzzle. You have a half-pound of metal (the op-rod) moving inside the rifle while the bullet is trying to stabilize. I don't care how good your "follow through" is; it can't overcome parts moving before they should.

This system was designed to shoot DRY (Fig 34)! Humidity is bad enough, but when you add a liquid like Hoppes, it will loosen up the carbon and turn it into a sticky paste. If you're in the middle of a string of slow fire and your shots are going wild, do the tilt test. If the piston is frozen, then yes, go ahead and use a few drops in the vent hole. This will get you through the match, but now is definitely an "As Needed" time to break down the system and clean out the carbon (Fig. 35).

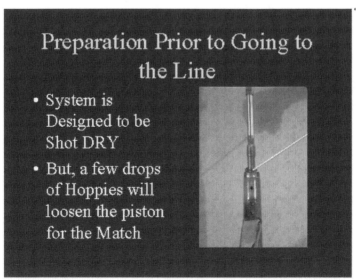

Fig. 34

Care, Cleaning & Sportsmanship

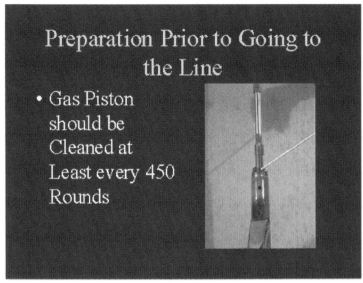

Fig. 35

You Can Do It

With a couple of special tools (see the source list), and with a few precautions, even we anvil manglers can get in and do a professional job of cleaning the gas system.

If you ignore step one, you will not harm the rifle, but you will give yourself some problems on the range you really don't want. Step one is to MARK the gas cylinder and plug (Fig. 36). When I first started shooting High Power in 1965, my gas cylinder plug came loose and my shots started to spray all over the target. I took my rifle to the armorer's van and they said my plug wasn't marked. After tightening the plug down, the armorer marked an index with a three-corner file. The next day's shooting revealed that I no longer had my usual zero. At 600 yards I had a ten-minute elevation change.

A fine brush and some white paint or some fingernail polish will do. Place an indexing mark on the gas cylinder plug, running it down and onto the gas cylinder. When the plug is loosened the marks will no longer align. After cleaning, you can tighten the plug down until the marks realign; your zero may change a little, but not ten minutes. *Marking the gas cylinder plug is step one.*

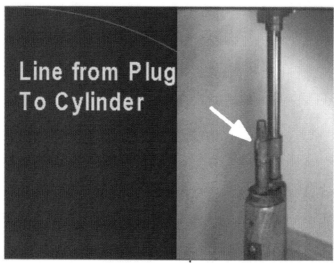

Fig. 36

If you choose to ignore step two, you may just as well go out and find a steamroller to run over your rifle. Attempting to remove the gas cylinder plug WITHOUT a gas cylinder wrench WILL destroy the accuracy of your rifle. Don't let this scare you away. A gas cylinder wrench is nothing more than an odd-shaped piece of metal designed to slip over your barrel and hold the gas system and the barrel in alignment while removing and replacing the plug. (See the source). Be careful to check prices, one place sells them for $27.50 and another sells one for $8.00. They both do the same job.

For you technocrats, the plug is placed on the rifle at 120 inch-pounds. It takes some force to break the plug free and again to reinstall it. Without the gas cylinder wrench you would be putting torque on the plug and would twist the gas system out of alignment with the barrel. *Using the gas cylinder wrench is step two.*

If you choose to ignore step three, don't bother cleaning the system in the first place. To clean the system you need to scrape the carbon out of the two reservoir halves: a) the gas cylinder plug and b) the piston. To do this you need another special tool. It is made of TWO drill bits: a letter "P" and a number "17" drill bit, epoxied into a wood handle. Some people use a handle on each drill bit; Charlie put one on each end of a single handle. You can make your own or see the source list to buy them. As a LAST resort you can use a 5/16ths and an 11/64ths drill bit. They are close to the right size but even a thousandth of an inch more carbon taken out with the proper size will do a better job.

The letter "P" drill bit is used to scrape out both the gas cylinder plug and part of the gas piston. The "r drill bit will clean only to the bottom of the thick portion of the gas piston. The reservoir actually goes down into the small stem of the gas piston. Use the number "17" drill bit to get down into the deeper tail area. *Getting at ALL the gunk* is step three.

To reassemble the gas system simply drop the piston into the gas cylinder. The tail end has a flat side and will fit only one way; you can't put it in wrong. Put your finger in the piston and turn. When the parts line up the piston will drop into place.

Install the piston DRY; no lube or grease. You should lightly lube the threads on the plug before replacing it. Remember to use the gas cylinder wrench and screw the plug down, making sure the index mark lines up. Do the tilt test and you're done.

The Hand Guard

Early April is as soon as we dare start Wednesday night practices here in Wisconsin. Even then, the trigger finger can start to freeze. We used to wrap our fingers around the smooth barrel as a hand warmer between slow fire shots. Later, when we changed barrels, Boots remarked, "Look at us, trying to warm our hands on a fluted barrel."

Warming your hands after a single shot is one thing, but grabbing hold of a hot barrel after a rapid fire string or, even worse, an M-14 after it has been fired full auto, can cook the skin right off your hand. "No one is dumb enough to grab a nearly red hot barrel," you say. Remember natural selection; it has been done.

The inventor of the M-14 must have known some really stupid people. He tried to prevent the problem by adding a hand "guard" to interfere with natural selection. I've seen the really dumb ones grab the hot barrel out past the gas system where there is no hand guard. Stupidity will find a way.

The hand guard on a "rack" gun is simply snapped into place and is free to move about one-eighth of an inch fore and aft. Take your fingers and lightly grip the edges of the hand guard and move it back and forth. A part of the rifle moving before the bullet leaves the barrel is not something to be desired.

A Match Conditioned M-14, M-1 or M1A has the hand guard glued into place to eliminate unwanted movement. "Care" is required in the handling of a match grade M1A or M-1. Picking up the rifle from the top, with the hand guard in the web between the thumb and forefinger, can cause the hand guard to loosen. If it's your rifle, your shots will spray all over the target. If it's someone else's rifle (and they see you pick it up like that) he can break your fingers and a jury of shooters will not convict.

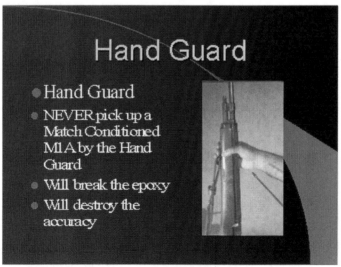

Fig. 37

Care, Cleaning & Sportsmanship

A Match Conditioned M-14, M-1 or M1A should always be picked up from <u>the underside</u>, near the upper sling swivel (See Fig 37).

If you go to Camp Perry and find you need your hand guard fixed, your trigger worked on, or your gas system cleaned, the Military Team Armorers will work on your rifle at no cost. They have to work on their team member's rifles first. They cannot supply parts but they are more than happy to help you.

The Stock Ferrule

Figure 38 shows the "Ferrule." This area needs to be free to move and should be lightly lubricated. When the rifle was built, the ferrule was polished smooth. At the end of a shooting season you may want to have your gunsmith check it and polish it with some crocus cloth. The gunsmith is a professional; don't try this at home (Charlie says: "Most folks figure, if anything is worth doing it is worth overdoing").

The ferrule is the band of metal on the stock that slides into the bracket (lower band) attached to the gas system. These two pieces of metal move slightly against each other and should be lubricated with a light coating of gun grease.

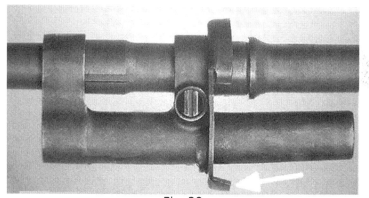

Fig. 38

Turn the rifle upside down and place the stock between your knees. Lay the barrel on your shooting stool, making sure the hand guard does not touch the stool. With a slight downward pressure on the stock, just behind the metal band, a small gap will form between the metal band and the bracket it slips into. Run a dry folded patch in the gap to clean out any dirt or grit. Now run a lightly greased patch in the gap and you're done. Do this each time you fire the rifle and make it a part of your care and cleaning.

The Spindle Valve

The spindle valve is the door in the passageway for the gases to travel from the barrel to the gas system. When the spindle valve is in the vertical position the door is open and the gases can pass through and the rifle fires semi-automatic. The piston, op-rod and bolt will operate. When the spindle valve is in the horizontal position, the door is closed and the gases will not operate the system. Only one shot at a time can be fired.

The purpose of the spindle valve is to close off the gas system to prevent damage to the rifle. Grenades are launched at a higher port pressure than conventional cartridges. Unless the local ordinances in your town permit the use of rifle grenades, leave the valve open. Charlie says on some M1As you can do damage by turning the valve; on many M1A/M14s the spindle becomes an integral part of the NM gas system. It is drilled and tapped to accept the assembly fasteners. Leave it alone.

Grandpa's Farm

When I was about five or six years old, I spent the summer on my Grandparents' farm. Alabama chickens LOVE to get into Grandma's garden, so she told me, "You catch him and we'll have chicken and dumplings for Supper."

All Summer I chased that little rascal. In the meantime I saw my Grandpa "Ring the neck" of a few chickens so "I" knew how to do it. Yep, you guessed it, one day I caught that rascal. His feet almost touched the ground each time he came around to the six o'clock position and he "did" go high over my head as I held onto his neck.

"Grandma, Grandma, we're going to have chicken and dumplings for Supper" I said.

She yelled, "PUT HIM DOWN, PUT HIM DOWN." I had never seen a chicken stagger before.

CHAPTER FOUR

MOLY COATING

The first half of this book was written about 1996. It was supposed to be ready for Camp Perry in Aug. 1997; I'm so glad it wasn't. I've learned so much that makes the old methods of care and cleaning obsolete*.

*Special note: during the editing process, Charlie took exception to a few of my comments and thought they needed expanding upon. Charlie says, "Doesn't make other methods obsolete - not everyone is using or will use moly. Use of moly will determine cleaning method needed, much the same as the different barrels and loads will affect cleaning methods and materials. These other methods aren't old and are needed to correctly care for equipment which is being used with industry standard match projectiles and conventional bore surfaces."

Now in 2015, I say "half the world swears by it and the other half swears at it." Today there are other methods that work as well or better than the Moly. Moly coating does have the advantages mentioned and is inexpensive and easy to apply.

The problem is some people believe you don't have to clean the barrel - You DO. They also believe the Moly itself protects the barrel - It DOES NOT.

Jim Owens
My Learning Process

I think the best way to approach this is to give it to you in a sort of chronological order as I have learned it.

Over the past year or so I kept hearing these words, like whispers on the wind; Moly, Moly Coating, Molied Bullets, Moly, Moly, Moly, Moly.

I saw my first Moly-coated bullet at Camp Perry. Thomas Whittaker had just won the National Championships. The next day, I was two targets down from him during the team match. The bullets were a purplish color and very shiny. So then I knew what they looked like, but that was all.

At Camp Perry I was introduced to Dave Emary, Chief Ballistics Scientist at Hornady Bullets®. Dave told me some interesting things about Moly coated bullets and what they can do for you. I will be referring back to our conversation because as you learn the wonderful properties of Moly coating from other credible sources, Dave's experiences gain a great deal of credibility, but more importantly, become additional confirmation.

At Camp Perry I interviewed seven National Champions, asking them how they cleaned their barrels. Naturally, I got seven different answers. The first half of David Tubbs answer opened my eyes (The full answer will be given later). "You know I Moly? I do not have to clean my barrel for 150 to 200 rounds" (without a loss of accuracy).

That was almost identical to what Dave Emary had told me a few days before. "You can go through a match like Camp Perry without cleaning the bore or with just a very light cleaning. "(Over-cleaning has a negative effect).

Walt Berger from BERGER BULLETS® told me, "Bench rest shooters normally clean the bore after every seven or eight rounds. With the Moly coated rounds, I'm cleaning after every eighty or one hundred rounds with no loss of accuracy, and you know how important accuracy is to us."

Dave does not recommend this for everyone, but he has tested up to 250 rounds without cleaning the bore, with no loss of accuracy. There is an unconfirmed story of one shooter firing up to 1,000 rounds of Moly coated bullets without cleaning the bore and with no loss of accuracy. Later I will show you WHY this can occur.

In the past I've learned that the advocates of Moly coating are claiming five wonderful things: 1) Longer barrel life, 2) Improved accuracy, 3) First shot accuracy, no fouling shots, 4) Longer times between cleaning with no loss of accuracy and 5) Cleaning of the bore is by far faster and easier.

Anything that sounds too good to be true usually is. NOW, I'M INTERESTED and I want to learn and find out, ARE THESE CLAIMS TRUE? I have heard people say "Don't say that (about 1-2-3-4 or 5). That hasn't been proven yet!"

As far as I'm concerned ALL FIVE CLAIMS ARE TRUE. I will attempt to share the best proof I have. I think we covered number four already. I'm not about to argue with David Tubb, Walt Berger and Hornady Ballistics Lab.

Let's take the remaining four claims: 1) Longer Barrel Life. Dave Emary from Hornady says he does not believe the claims of 2 to 3 times longer barrel life. He thinks its maybe 25 - 30%. In my book 25% is a significant amount, and well worth the effort to moly.

Now let's look at the other end of that stick. Uncle Bob works for a large gun manufacturer and he says in their test with molyed bullets they are getting (with some barrels) 2 - 3 times less throat erosion. He says this is caliber dependent. The .223 caliber is by far the best, the .30 caliber barrels have a significant increase and the belted magnums have a slight increase in barrel life. The test showed the best results came from cryo treated, high quality barrels.

Locally, Dave Hickey is our resident expert on the AR-15 and he keeps excellent records. He says that during the 1992 shooting season, before he molyed his bullets, he was firing 52 gr. bullets at 200 yards, 69 gr. at 300 yards and 80 gr. at 600 yards. Over a period of 3357 rounds he was getting about 61 rounds per one thousandth of an inch throat erosion.

In 1997, using molyed bullets, he started with a new barrel; same type, same caliber, same chamber, same barrel maker, same gunsmith and same powder (WW 748). He used only 69 gr. bullets for 2 & 3 hundred yards and 80 gr. for 600 yards. In 1,031 rounds, he was getting about 208 rounds per one thousandth of an inch throat erosion. 208 divided by 61 is 3.4. OK, you decide: 25% on the small end or 3.4 times less throat erosion on the high side. In either case, I think it is worth the time and effort.

Now let's talk about claim number 2): Improved Accuracy. Back to the conversation with Dave Emary in the pits at Camp Perry. He said, "You will notice your groups will be more round, with fewer fliers and possibly tighter." (Note, you have to do your job for the molyed bullets to do their job. Throwing your shoulder into the rifle, miss-aligning the sights or jerking the trigger will not help).

Boots Obermeyer has a 6.5 mm barrel with about 4,500 rounds on it. He started to shoot molyed bullets, and won a 4-gun 600 match at Eau Claire, Wisconsin this summer with a score of 798 out of the possible 800. Big Deal, he'd done that plenty of times. BUT, his X count this time was 63 X's. He says his groups are rounder and smaller.

I just started shooting the Hornady 75 gr. A-Max® bullets, molyed. I shot a 4-gun 600 match. The first two strings were with Iron Sights and I had a lot of elevation problems. The third string was with the scope and I had a 200-9X. Big Deal, BUT, I noticed in my data book, all the shots outside the X ring were JUST out (Fig 39). If the X ring had been another inch to an inch and a half, I would have had a 200 with 17 X's. I know, if a frog had wings, he wouldn't bump his butt every time he jumped.

Care, Cleaning & Sportsmanship

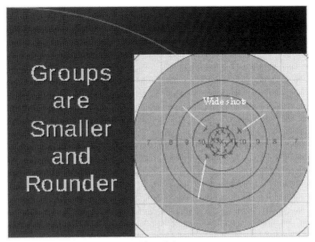
Fig. 39

A couple of our Expert-class shooters have found their accuracy is better with the molyed bullets. They are getting 200's at 600 yards and 100 with 5 X's at 300 rapid. They are happy.

Point 3): First shot accuracy, no fouling shots. Grant Ubl is on the Wisconsin Eagle Team (They won the Civilian Combat Infantry Trophy Match at Camp Perry in 1995 and 1996, missed 1997 by a few points and won again in 1998). He is also on the 1999 U.S. Palma Team. In other words, a damn good long range shooter.

Grant has been shooting Molyed bullets for over a year now and he wanted to see how his first shot accuracy was at long range. He just finished a Palma Match and had about sixty rounds down the bore. He used his cleaning method (covered later) and the next day fired a Thousand Yard Match. His first shot was right where he finished the day before, just above the X-ring. His second shot was right through the spotter and the next three shots were in the same spot.

Police (SWAT Teams) MUST have the first shot right on the money; they don't get sighting or fouling shots. They call it their "Cold Bore Zero." I believe that eventually the Police will be using the Molyed bullets for this point alone.

George Lainhart is a SWAT/Sniper Instructor on the City of College Park Police Department in College Park, Ga. He says with the Molyed bullets his "Cold Bore Zero" is on each and every time. He says that Bert Medina, the Chief Firearms Instructor for the U.S. Customs Agency, is using Moly coated bullets. George says that Norma and Blackhills Ammunition Companies are producing Moly bullets for the Police. If you are a Police officer and would like a fellow officer's views, give George a call at 770-964-7028.

We have already covered point 4): Longer times between cleaning with no loss of accuracy. So let's move on to point 5): Cleaning of the bore is far faster and easier. That is the point of this book and it will be covered as we go along, and after learning some fundamentals.

The next large step in my education came in the fall of 1997 when I saw an ad in Shooting Sports USA for a product called Ms. Moly®, Ballistic Conditioner, an aerosol spray Moly (1-800-264-4140, for technical support or questions call 414-763-8687).

I noticed the company was in Burlington, Wisconsin about a forty-five minute drive from me, so I called and talked to Dave Brown, the man in charge. Dave invited me down and gave me a complete run through on both Moly in general and his product in particular.

I didn't know Dave Brown, so I was skeptical. He had two things in his favor. The first and most important thing he had going was a booklet from Dow Corning® called "Illustrated Mechanism of Molybdenum Disulfide Lubrication." This is a series of pictures taken under an electron microscope. The second thing he had going for him was the fact that he demonstrated his product and it did what he said it would. Both convinced me that molying both the bullet and the bore is absolutely the way to go. His product has a better way to do this (in some respects) than powered moly.

Before we get started let's get a few things straight. We are talking about Molybdenum Disulfide. I'm not typing THAT

Care, Cleaning & Sportsmanship

18,000 times, so I will only say 'Moly.' The same goes for MoS2, the abbreviation for Molybdenum Disulfide, again because of the trouble I would have to go through each time with the small 2, I will just call it 'Moly.'

Keep in mind Dow Corning will be mentioning lubricants, pastes, oils, greases, and bonded coatings. Moly has been adapted for shooting without the need of other elements.

Space prevents me from running their entire book and the second half is so technical most of us wouldn't under-stand it. Dow Corning sent me a photocopy since the original book is out of print. I reduced the pictures to fit here. They will give you an understanding of how 'Moly' works. After the pictures, I talk about how this applies to a barrel and bullets.

The opening page states in part: "The problems of friction and lubrication are mainly surface problems and the scanning electron microscope is an excellent tool for studying the surfaces of solids. 'Moly', a solid and a lubricant, is an ideal subject for study. The features of scanning electron microscope that make it so ideal studying the mechanism of lubrication of 'Moly' are:

1. Magnification up to 20,000X.
2. Direct examination of the surface without pretreatment, which might ruin important information.
3. Depth of focus that gives three dimensional information in single pictures.

These advantages are particularly useful in studying the mechanism of 'Moly'. The following sequence of pictures tells its own story with the help of only a few words of explanation."

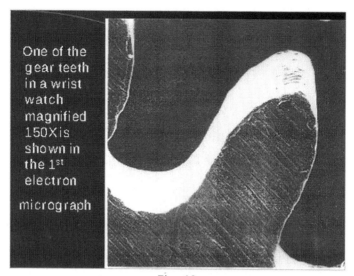

Fig. 40

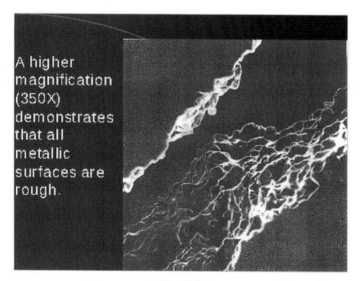

Fig. 41

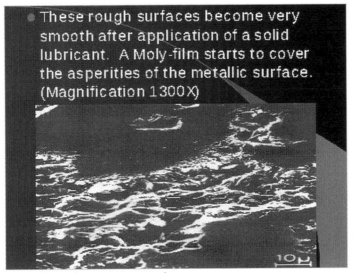

Fig. 42

THE FOLLOWING SERIES OF 8 PICTURES SHOWS THE LUBRICATION PROCESS OF MOLYBDENUM DISULFIDE FROM A LOOSE POWDER TO A STRONGLY ADHERING SMOOTH FILM ON A METAL SURFACE.

Fig. 43

Fig. 44

Fig. 45

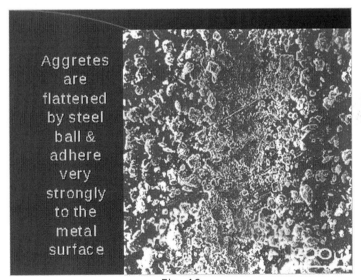
Fig. 46

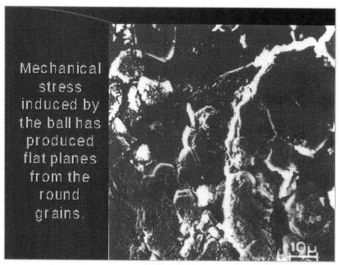

Fig. 47

Fig. 48

At still higher magnification (Figure 46) it is seen that the lamella (thin plate) layers of 'Moly' single crystals are pushed apart by the mechanical stress of the steel ball. Easy sliding of layers and adhesion provide 'Moly' with excellent film forming properties. (My comments: The 'Moly' shingles out in this process. It's much like taking a deck of cards on a table and applying pressure with your hand. If you push the cards to the far side of the table, the cards will shingle, one overlapping the other. Look closely at the flattened particle in the center (shaped like an arrow head), and you can see this shingling effect.)

Figure 48 shows the result of the sliding action of the ball after several passes over the same area is to cause the 'Moly' platelets to spread out and cover more of the steel surface.

When a smooth 'Moly' - film is formed on the metal surface, no more sliding of Moly' - layers is observed. This thin coating protects the metal surfaces from wear and provides them with a smooth solid lubricant film.

Fig. 49

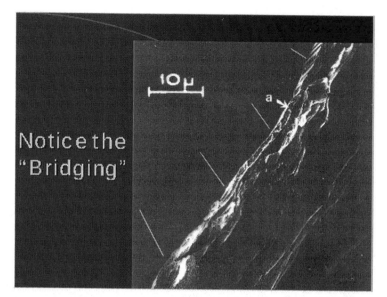

Fig. 50

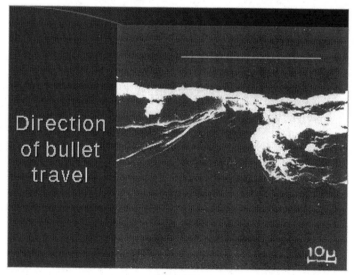

Fig. 51

In Figure 50 we see a cross-section of the 'Moly'-coated metal surface. A thin, solid 'Moly' film (a) of 2 microns thickness adheres to the surface and prevents metal to metal contact, thus reducing friction and wear. (My comments: Notice the shingled 'Moly' has formed a bridge from one high point to the next, not filling in the low spots).

In Figure 51, a single asperity of a sandblasted metal surface was plastically deformed underneath the 'Moly' - film. As the surface roughness is reduced, the area of contact beneath the 'Moly' film is increased. Therefore, the load is distributed over a larger area . . . No Seizure . . . No abrasive wear.

There is one section in the rest of the book that shows and explains that the 'Moly' film makes a hardened zone three times harder than the metal itself.

CONCLUSIONS

The excellent lubricating properties of 'Moly' are due: To the ease of sliding of 'Moly' - lamellae.

To the good adhesion of these lamellae to metal surfaces.

To the ability of these lamellae to form a homogeneous thin film.

This film has a very low coefficient of friction and withstands pressures exceeding 500,000 psi.

(**My comments:** In other parts of the book that I could not get to because of space limits, they showed that the Moly film only builds to a, certain thickness and does not grow any thicker. Dave Brown said "Moly either burnishes into the metal or it goes out the bore, it does not accumulate and it does not foul.")

My Comments: If you 'Moly' coat your barrel and bullets, you will no longer have metal to metal contact. There will be no high spots to tear copper jackets from the bullets. The copper fouling is greatly reduced and cleaning the barrel is extremely easy.

Jim Owens

Spray Moly

After Dave Brown showed me the Dow Corning book and the pictures under the electron microscope, he said a few things that made sense. "When people moly coat their bullets with powder, then they have to transfer that moly to the bore by firing twenty rounds or so (after completely cleaning out all of the old copper and carbon fouling)."

Dave continued "As you fire the first of those twenty rounds, moly is deposited on the bore just ahead of the throat by an inch or so, then the next round deposits another inch or so down the barrel. The heat and pressure shingles the moly and forms the bridge across the high points of the metal." Photo in Fig. 48.

He asked, "What happens in front of the area that has been molyed as the bullet travels down the bore?" I replied, "You are depositing copper and carbon fouling ahead of each molyed section." "Right," he said, "and you are molying right over it."

"Spray moly is about one twentieth the size of powdered moly. It is suspended in a distillate that evaporates off quickly, if the barrel or bullets are warmed to about 150 degrees or warm to the touch; by the sun, a hair dryer, a heat gun or in the oven."

Dave said, "The small particles of the spray moly make them ideal for conditioning the bore. Picture a gravel road up close. The roughness is much like the picture in Fig. 41. When it starts to snow, the low spots are filled in first and the snow builds up until the high spots are covered. Now when a car drives over the road, it packs down the snow. Then several cars drive over the area. Pretty soon, the road is smooth as glass. You don't have to worry about excess, because the moly will burnish into the metal or go out the bore."

"The reason you moly your bullets is to keep the moly from wearing out in the barrel. If you shot non-molyed bullets down a molyed barrel, you would transfer the moly from the barrel to the bullets and eventually wear down to the high spots and re-deposit copper fouling."

My Comments: I talked to a lot of people and got comments both for and against conditioning the bore. Jack Krieger, Charlie Milazzo* and Dow Corning all said, "Conditioning the bore is a better way to go."

*Charlie says "If you're going to use moly it is the logical way to start. But not everyone is going to be able to use and stick with moly right now. Eventually it will probably become the standard. For those who do not have access to moly coated bullets or approved factory loaded ammo, moly coating of the bore proves to be nothing more than the introduction of a variable into the accuracy equation. Consider carefully before firing any moly coated bullets through a barrel which will primarily be used with standard uncoated projectiles, or before coating the bore with moly. For some folks that introduced random unknown could eat you alive. Consistency is the key to dependable accuracy. Changing bore conditions compromises, at the very least, any consistency."

"There is going to be a transition period with molyed bullets. Where everything will be in flux. This is it! There's going to be a lot of wild claims and most likely some problems. We can only try to recognize the possibilities before they occur to help reduce or eliminate the stumbling. How do I feel about moly? I think it has tremendous potential."

Moly Snobs

During my talks to all these different people, I coined a phrase, "Moly Snob." People who are already using powdered moly did not even want to hear of spray moly. They didn't want to put anything in their bore (Sorry Bubba, you ARE putting moly in your bore when you shoot the powdered bullets). "I don't want to condition my bore." Again, you ARE conditioning your bore with the powdered molyed bullets, you are just doing it inefficiently.

Moly Snobs remind me of the people who say: "My Chevy truck is better than your Ford truck and I'll put on the decal of the little boy peeing on your logo to prove it."

People have their own cleaning techniques and ideas of molying to the point of dogma and/or religion. They will (verbally) fight to the death to prove "My Moly is better than your moly."

Back to Dave Brown's demonstration. He then showed me how to use his product "Ms. Moly" on a barrel. You need to warm the object, barrel or bullets, first. Warming them evaporates the distillates quickly and the moly dries instantly.

He has as part of the kit a couple pieces of polyethylene with a series of holes punched in rows. He calls them the "wholly organizer." You simply set the organizer on a flat surface like a pane of glass and drop the warmed bullets into the holes. When the organizer is full, lift it up and off.

What remains is row on row of bullets standing at attention like a platoon of soldiers ready for inspection. You then shake the can of "Ms. Moly" and spray; front, back, right and left. You may want to give a second coat from the four corners.

I immediately picked up one of the bullets and it was dry; no moly came off on my hand. Powdered moly is messy, but washes up with soap and water. Dave said, "Try to scrape it off with your finger nail." I tried and could not.

A friend was at a match and a Sgt. on the Marine Corps Team asked to look at his molyed bullets. He scraped some off with his fingernail and told Andy, "You have to tumble them longer. The moly should not scrape off."

How Do You Moly The Bore?

Dave Brown suggests you first try it on a shotgun barrel because it is so much bigger and you can see what's going on. He recommends you place a patch or cotton ball in one end. If you are dumb enough to do this over your wife's carpet, you are a candidate for natural selection.

Again, heat the barrel until it is warm to the touch. Hold the barrel so the bead is up or at the 12 o'clock position. Shake the can of moly and give a two second spray down the barrel. Turn the sight down to the 6 o'clock position and give another two second spray. Do this again at the 3 & 9 o'clock positions.

Remove the patch or cotton ball and place it in the end you just sprayed. Repeat the procedure from the other end, 12-6-3 and 9 o'clock positions. Now look down the bore and you will see the moly start to weep or run. Now brush the bore to burnish the moly into the barrel. This is the first application; you need to give it three applications.

I looked down the bore of the shotgun barrel and it was very bright. Dave Brown said, "Turn it around and look down the other end." When I did my head snapped back.

The bore was So bright, it was like being hit with a spot-light in a dark room.

I also noticed some little black beads in the bore (the barrel had been previously fired). It seems the carbon fouling beads up much like rain drops on a polished and waxed car. They are hard, black beads and you would have to be blind not to see them. After a rifle match, I took the lower receiver off to reduce the weight. I placed a clean, white patch near the chamber and held it up to the shop light. The reflected light down the bore showed the black beads of carbon fouling. After cleaning, I could see the two beads I had missed.

Defending the Lady's Honor

I was told by one of our regular shooters "Ms. Moly spray has graphite in it and should not be used." As proof he Faxed me a Material Safety Data Sheet from Dow Corning for Dow Corning 321 Dry Film Lubricant (Aerosol)®. Yes, it has 3% graphite.

I called David Brown and asked if he re-labeled Dow Corning 321 Dry Film Lubricant (Aerosol) as his own "Ms. Moly." He told me no, that his spray is made for shooting, with no graphite. He then Faxed me his Material Safety Data Sheet on "Ms. Moly" showing there is no graphite.

The next assault on the Lady's honor came when several people decided there had to be some "Binders" in the spray to make the moly stick to the bullets. Again, the Material Safety Data Sheet rode to the rescue; no binders.

This did alert us to the fact that some spray molys have graphite in them. You don't want graphite in your bore, because it's an abrasive.

I part company with one thing Dave Brown said, "It's OK to moly the chamber." A lot of people say NO and some say yes. Boots said it probably would be all right, but Charlie says, "Boots knows what he is doing when it comes to loading. There are a lot of people who may not recognize the fact that they could get into some serious trouble. Reduced friction between the brass and chamber wall equals increased thrust on the bolt face and locking lugs."

If you are going to spray the moly into the breach end, use the rod guide with the "O" ring to keep the moly away from the chamber. You can spray a patch or mop, then apply it to the bore and burnish it in with the bronze brush.

Another Method

NECO MOLY-SLIDE® is a paste and comes in a one ounce plastic tube. It contains no graphite. It contains approximately 60% laboratory-grade, extremely small, micron-sized Moly in paste form. It takes a VERY small amount to go a long way. Some people are using the NECO MOLY-SLIDE® to condition the bore and to touch up after cleaning to eliminate the need for fouling shots after over-cleaning. You can order the NECO MOLY-SLIDE® direct from NECO, 800-451-3550 or from O.K. Weber.

Removing Moly

Someone told me you cannot remove the moly once it is placed in the bore. When I told Dave Brown that, he showed me a new product he will soon have available. He sprayed it on a molyed bullet and it instantly removed all the moly. I have since learned MEK, methyl ethyl ketone, will do the same thing and you can get it at the hardware store.

2015 update; a new product:

Fig. 52

BORE TECH MOLY MAGIC

Molybdenum disulfide (commonly referred to as 'Moly') is a substantive material, which means that it clings to metal surfaces readily, and while this is part of the mechanism which allows moly to provide friction reduction, it also makes it difficult to remove with traditional bore cleaning solvents.

In the presence of high temperatures and high pressures, moly breaks down, causing a thick build-up and a corrosive sulfuric acid byproduct. Both residues can significantly decrease accuracy and destroy barrel steel if not appropriately cleaned.

Bore Tech's MOLY MAGIC penetrates deep into the metal's pores while a specially formulated surfactant system that suspends and attracts the particles to the patch with electrostatic force, greatly increasing cleaning efficiency. MOLY MAGIC is not a bore cleaner, and should be used in conjunction with a bore cleaner like Bore Tech's ELIMINATOR to achieve proper cleaning results.

Avail. from: Jim Owens (Jarheadtop.com), Amazon.com, Sinclair International

My Conclusions on Spray Moly

Spray moly will not replace powdered moly! It simply cannot compete economically. I have been told the 4 oz. of industrial (1 micron) powdered moly will do 20,000 to 40,000 rounds. The 10 oz. bottle of regular (5 micron) moly will do 50,000 to 100,000 rounds for under $35.00.

For conditioning the bore, the spray moly or NECO Molyslide® paste is "The better way to go." It is faster and cleaner than powdered moly. If a person lives in an area without a workshop, basement, etc., like an apartment, the spray is ideal.

When we go shopping for our food, if we want something fast and easy to prepare, we are willing to pay more. If we want economy, we buy things that will take time and effort to prepare. It's all a tradeoff.

Spray and powder each have their place and can co-exist. I believe the spray is best for conditioning the bore and quick and easy for molying bullets when you are in a hurry or small quantities of bullets or fixed ammo which do not merit all the trouble of tumbling. Powder is best for the long haul economics.

Powdered Moly

Guns and Ammo magazine ran an article called "21st - Century Accuracy" by Tom Gresham. It said, in part:

> **Bullet breakthroughs**
> A bullet-coating process developed by (NECO) Nostalgia Enterprises Company (510/450-0420) involves tumbling bullets to "impact plate" them with Molybdenum Disulfide, then following up with a coat of carnauba wax. The

result: greater accuracy, reduced friction, reduced bore - fouling and, in some cases, reduced bullet - drop—with the same velocity. Walt Berger, president of Berger Bullets (602/842-4001), said his bench rest rifle now has more than 800 Moly-coated rounds through it without having seen a brush—he cleans with only a wet patch and a dry patch. NECO offers kits for do-it-yourselfers; Berger will Moly-coat any of his bullets for an additional charge of only $2 to $4 per 100 bullets. "Within two years," he says, "every ammunition company will have to offer Moly-coated bullets."

This article was taken off the Internet and was mailed to me by the gentleman at Dow Corning. The phone numbers in the article opened new doors in my quest for information. I called NECO and talked to Roger Johnson, the man in charge. After introducing myself and telling him about this book, I had some questions and some "feedback" for him.

I asked "How much does your kit cost?" He replied: "$137.35." (I have seen them advertised for $148.00 from other distributors). I then asked "What does the kit include?" He said "1) a 4 oz. jar of one micron Moly powder, 2) 13 1/2 lbs. of 5/32 Dia. ground steel balls, heat treated to Rockwell C50, 3) 3 oz. of carnauba wax, 4) a sample bullet and 5) a complete instruction manual."

I told him, I had some feed-back from shooters who are using powdered Moly, some with his kits and they are not using the wax. In fact, some are warning against using the wax because it is causing problems. He said, "We have not heard of any problems and the people who are giving up on the wax don't know what they are losing. Norma says that they get 10 - 35% better ballistics depending on the barrel."

He has a product called Moly-Slide (I picked up a tube from O.K. Weber at Camp Perry in 1997). Roger said that he will condition a new bore with the Moly Slide by putting some on a patch and running it down the bore. It is also good if you get over aggressive in your cleaning and take the Moly out of the bore. A touch up will re-Moly the bore and you don't need the extra bullets to do the job.

Roger told me something else that I found interesting. With products that have ammonia in them like Sweets, he neutralizes them with water. He then dry patches the bore and protects it with oil. The oil must be cleaned out before you shoot the next time.

One thing Roger told me of which I was not aware. **Moly DOES NOT protect the bore from moisture and humidity.** He uses a light coat of oil while storing the rifle, again cleaning out the bore before shooting the next time.

<u>Update: Now days half the people swear by Moly and the other half swear at it. It seems some people did not protect the bore and problems did occur and they blamed the Moly.</u>

Midway's Kit

Midway (800)-243-3220 has a Deluxe Pack (8 oz. Moly & 2 #1292 hard plastic bowls) #610-434 for $34.99. They also have their Ultimate Pack, a #1292 Tumbler with an extra bowl and 8 oz. of Moly, #480-460 for $69.99. Check for current prices.

When I called to ask them about their kit, they told me they don't use the steel balls, as the bullets themselves do the impacting. OK, I need to know, "Does this work?" I called a friend because I knew he just bought a tumbler, Moly and some steel balls and was going to run his first batch that evening. He said he would try them without the steel balls. The next day he called and told me he ran 1,000 of the 69 gr. bullets and they came out perfect. The following day he called back saying he ran 1,600 of the 69 gr. bullets and again they came out perfect.

OK, How did he do it? He simply put the bullets in the tumbler and added 4 oz. of Moly and ran them for two hours. After shutting the tumbler off he used a slotted serving spoon to pick up the bullets and sift out the Moly. He then placed them in an old sock to rub off the excess Moly (a towel or paper

Care, Cleaning & Sportsmanship

towel works fine). Then he put the bullets in a ZipLoc® bag or back in their original boxes. You can add a little Moly to each new batch or run the Moly that's in the tumbler until its gone. (OOOPS, I just talked to Midway and asked them how they did it. I liked their answer better; they use 1/8 teaspoon of Moly for each five pounds of bullets). Fast, Simple, Easy, and Inexpensive. Powdered Moly is messy, but it cleans up with soap and water.

Another update:
The Best way to Moly .223 Bullets

This is the fastest, easiest, least messy and least expensive way to Moly your bullets. Most people shoot the .223 rounds.

Get a pill bottle (One that holds 500 Ibuprofen). This bottle is the perfect size to hold 100 rounds of .223 heads.

After pouring the bullets into the bottle, without touching them, simply put in the Moly.

Here is the best part. "How much Moly do I use?"

Get yourself a set of measuring spoons. Use the 1/8 teaspoon. *Do NOT* use the whole 1/8 teaspoon. Put just a tiny bit on the tip of the spoon and already you have used way too much.

Close the cap and place in the tumbler. If you have the bottle with a screw on cap, place the cap to the right. If you place the cap to the left, it will unscrew and the bullets will fall out. Tumble the bottle for two hours.

Take a shop rag and lay it on the bench. Pour the heads onto the rag and fold it over and roll the heads around. The rag will soak up the excess Moly. Dump the heads onto a second clean shop rag and repeat the process. The second rag will soak up the remaining excess and will clean the heads.

Now pour them back into the box. The bullets come out perfect and there is no mess.

If you shoot a larger caliber, a Peanut Butter jar works just fine.

Sources of Moly

Here is a list of places I know of to get Moly that will do the job. 1) NECO, (510) 450- 0420 has a 4 oz. container of ultra-fine (1 micron) Moly #MC-12 for $42.75. 2) Dow Corning has a 10 oz. bottle of 5 micron Moly called "Z-Powder." They do not sell directly to the public but if you call them at (517) 496-6000 they will give you the name of a company in your area that caries the Z-Powder. In Milwaukee it was Wisconsin Bearing and they sold the 10 oz. bottle for $32.86. 3) Midway (800) 243-3220 buys the Z-Powder in large quantities and sells an 8 oz. jar #677-866 for $19.99. Now you need a rotary tumbler or a vibrator tumbler; either will work fine. Check or current prices.

Joe Blow Schmuckatelly

Joe asked me not to mention his real name (in fact, Joe is a composite of 4 or 5 different people). Joe said that he found with the NECO kit's instructions they have a ratio of bullet weight to steel ball weight. He simply used a 12 oz. coffee mug to weigh the bullets. A few 180 grs., or a lot of 69 gr. bullets come out to the proper ratio. He says the coffee mug works great. So, fill your coffee mug with bullets and level off the top. Pour the bullets into the steel balls, add a squirt of Moly (about 1/8th teaspoon) and let it run for a couple of hours. Joe says he uses a plastic pail with holes drilled in the bottom to separate the bullets from the steel balls; a Dillon media separator works also.

Now put the bullets on a terry cloth towel (paper towels work) and rub off the excess Moly. You should not be able to scratch off the Moly with your finger nail.

Andy Ladron called and said, "It doesn't work. I ran them for two hours, added more Moly then ran them another two hours, then added more Moly again and again." He has a tumbler with a rubber liner. The Moly was soaking into the rubber. You need a tumbler made of hard plastic.

Do You Have To Clean The Bullets Before Molying?

If you are using Hornady bullets (not seconds), just dump them right in the bowl. DO NOT touch them first, the oils on your hands will prevent the Moly adhering to the bullets. Some people have acidic sweat and the Moly will not stick. If you have to handle the bullets first, use cotton gloves. Some of the other bullet makers have a film on the bullets that must be removed before you can Moly them. Running the bullets in a corn cob media will clean them or you could try MEK or acetone. (Again, OOOPS, I just talked to Midway and they said you can run the bullets in Dawn dish washing soap and water to remove the grease, then air dry them).

How do I clean the bore and break in the barrel?

Two very important questions, with the usual thousand answers. The one I like best came from Berger Bullets (Questions & Answers) @ http/www.bergerbullets.com/faq.htm. Reprint follows:

Q. How do I clean my rifle using Moly Coated bullets?

The best procedure for cleaning when using Moly coated bullets is as follows:

   1. Two wet patches with Kroil.
   2. One patch with JB bore cleaner. Short stroke the patch from the breach to the muzzle.
   3. Two wet patches with Kroil.
   4. Two dry patches.

This procedure is suggested after approximately 80 to 100 rounds, depending on the class of rifle being fired.

Q. How do I break in a barrel with Moly Coated bullets?

The procedure that Walt has found to be the best is as follows:

1. Run a wet patch of Kroil through the barrel.
2. Fire one shot then clean using our cleaning procedure.
3. Repeat step 2 two more times.
4. Fire 3 shot groups 5 times cleaning after every 3 shots. Your barrel will now be broken in.

What is Kroil and where do you get it?

When I asked that question, I was told, "It's a penetrating oil you can get anywhere." "OK, the next time you're at McDonalds, pick up a can," I said. "You can get it at any auto parts or hardware store." Oh yeah, three auto parts stores and two hardware stores later, I got tired of hearing "We never heard of it." (Avail from Jim Owens at Jarheadtop.com, Amazon.com, Sinclair International) The first time I heard of Kroil was when Mid Tomkins told me he uses 50% Kroil and 50% Shooters Choice as his bore cleaner (other shooters have said they use 2 parts Hoppes to 1 part Kroil).

Another Cleaning Method

Another cleaning method came from Grant Ubl. He runs a couple of wet patches soaked in Shooters Choice down the bore. Then with a plastic or nylon brush wet with Shooters Choice, he scrubs the bore. He will then dry patch the bore. Here is the interesting part, he says you will never stop getting black from the Moly, but he will run an EXTREMELY tight patch down the bore until he gets minimal amounts of black on the patch.

The above method is used when he has to shoot the next day (remember, over aggressive cleaning removes the moly). When he has unlimited sighters, (to re-moly the bore) and wants to get a little more aggressive, he uses the following method: He runs several wet patches with regular Shooters Choice, followed by Shooters Choice Copper Remover. Dry patch, then he uses JB Bore Cleaner to scrub the bore, followed by wet patches of Shooters Choice to flush the JB, then dry patches. He says he'll need 6-8 rounds to re-moly and all is right with the world.

A Word of Caution

Dave Emary from Hornady called and told me some of the 50 cal. shooters are reporting that some of the moly has sulfur in it and the bore cleaners with ammonia is forming a chemical reaction that is etching the bore. I was offered some moly and I checked the Material Safety Data Sheet; it had 40% sulfur. I said, "No Thanks."

A Passing Fad?

One of the Moly Snobs said "This Moly Coating is a passing fad and everyone is jumping on the band wagon." He doesn't like to try anything new until it's been around for fifty years or so.

I have personally seen increased accuracy and easier cleaning with Moly coated bullets. I know someone who keeps excellent records, showing less throat erosion (longer barrel life). I talked to long range shooters and Police Officers (SWAT) who say the first shot is right there. I have talked to experts in the field who say one can shoot more rounds between cleanings before accuracy drops off.

If only one of these is true, move over; I'm coming aboard this band wagon!!!

CHAPTER FIVE

I put out a letter to my mailing list asking, "If you could ask Boots Obermeyer, Jack Kreiger, Charlie Milazzo or Mike Bykowski a question, what would it be??" Many of the questions were identical and many were similar. I combined some of them into one. I broke them into categories. Here are their answers, for your enjoyment:

Barrel

Q. What is the fundamental, always works, cleaning routine?
Charlie: "I prefer Hoppe's #9. Wet bore with solvent - let time do the work, it's the safest. Not always practical due to time constraints. Store with bore wet."

Boots: "I use Hoppes BR; if heavy fouling or very wet residue use Remclean. If big problem with copper use Sweets. In my testing, using sections of well used bores, I found carbon fouling difficult to remove, normal cleaners just won't do it. Best way was abrasive particle cleaners like Remclean or JB Bore cleaner."

Q. Which chemicals can be mixed or can't be mixed?
Charlie: "To be on the safe side don't mix any, there is no reason to—but, ammonia base with other ammonia base is usually OK."

Boots: "Don't mix Sweets with Shooters Choice! I have seen etching from resulting 3rd chemical, so did Sal at Venco."

Q. Pros & Cons of using a Teflon additive to the bore?

Charlie: "Pro: supposedly slipperier surface, this slippery surface is supposed to reduce fouling, increase velocity, reduce wear, reduce the national debt, etc. etc. Con: It is a variable. It can eventually be shot or cleaned out of the bore. At that time the bore condition has changed. It's difficult to determine interval or effect of change in bore condition."

Q. Can regular car oil (10W 40) be used in a rifle bore?

Charlie: "Only if you change the filter and use a lighter oil in the winter ?????? Yes engine oil will act as a rust inhibitor, but so will Hoppe's #9 AND it will eat copper deposits at the same time."

Boots: "If you are short of Hoppes and need corrosion protection it's better than nothing. May develop a sludge due to oil additives."

Q. Best method for cleaning a fouled out barrel?

Charlie: "Solvent - solvent - solvent - solvent & time. It works on any barrel."

Boots: "Soak with Hoppes BR overnight, next day use Remclean —put on patch wrapped around a brush, scrub out & dry patch."

Q. Does soaking for prolonged periods 6 - 8 days (Shooters Choice & Hoppe's) w/patching 2 times daily harm the barrel?

Charlie: "If you mix the two it will. Meaning of SOAK: 1) wet the bore with a patch - OK, 2) fill the bore with solvent - NO. On a gas gun the solvent will enter the port and gas system; also there is too much chance of damage from leakage. That much solvent can leak & really mess up the bedding. Also continued recycling of the solvent will degrade the solvent by decreasing the potency of the solution—via chemical neutralization."

Boots: "I agree, mixing Hoppes with Shooters Choice can cause problems, same as with Sweets. My test years ago showed Shooters Choice the least effective of the cleaners—zip on copper—I haven't used their new Copper Cleaner. If cleaning with a strong ammonia cleaner like Sweets, be careful not to leave it in the bore for a long period of time, it may become an electrolyte and etch the bore. Sweets only takes five minutes to start working and is depleted by fifteen minutes, clean it out."

Q. Does using spray brake cleaner solvent harm the barrel? "Sure cuts glazing."
Charlie: "Shouldn't hurt, but it removes ALL rust preventatives - do not store this way. Be careful - this could harm the bedding or stock finish."

Q. Do coatings like S&W Friction Block harm the barrel? Seems to reduce fouling.
Charlie: "See Teflon additive above. How long do they last? How do you know when it's going away? What effect on accuracy as surface changes? Primary problem is that you introduce a random variable into your accuracy equation. This will happen on Match Day, you know, Murphy's Law."

Boots: "Only used on trigger parts."

Q. How much brushing is enough or too much to damage the barrel?
Charlie: "One stroke - with the wrong brush. A few strokes with the wrong rod or techniques. Many, many if done properly - but infinitely less than just patching, before damage occurs or becomes evident. Damage = A reduction in the accurate life span of the barrel - some of this damage can be minuscule - but if damage occurs from your normal cleaning procedure - it WILL be progressive. Cleaning should enhance accuracy and prolong the accurate life span of the barrel. Proper techniques should maintain the quality of the barrel while reducing or eliminating the potential for damage. Doing nothing WILL destroy the barrel, too."

Boots: "Stressed surface of bore may actually be attacked more by a brush than particle cleaners - saw this on tests using a microscope. I use to clean if needed in the match, a few strokes. Dry cleaning gives less zero shift. Cleaning may have some wear on bore, particles or brush. So does shooting. Particles tend to smooth surface and give some increase in life. One worry, Crown may wear some and need to be redone."

Q. Do stainless steel barrels require different methods of cleaning than regular steel?
Charlie: "Usually high quality stainless steel barrels clean easier than chrome moly. Chrome moly does not mean chrome plated."

Boots: "Stainless scratches easier than Chrome Moly even if they have the same Rockwell hardness. Must be very carefully cleaned. Throat erosion is a different nature. Large flat areas look like a dried up mud puddle. Chrome Moly is like pebbles and will pick up more fouling."

Q. Which powders shoot the cleanest and do the least amount of damage (erosion)? Single or double based powders? Foreign or domestic powders?
Boots: "Ball propellants usually foul more due to coating to reduce burning. Not much difference between single or double based powders. Only Winchester ball is domestic."

Q. Is it OK to wipe Teflon w/oil, plain oil, or Hoppes bore cleaner, on the bullet just prior to firing the round? The oil products for lubricating the bore OR the bore cleaner for helping clean the bore.
Charlie: "I wouldn't—how do you establish and/or maintain any consistency by introducing these variables? Accuracy is only found through consistency or blind luck."

Mike: "NO! You should not have any kind of material wiped on either the case or the bullet that could track any extraneous material into the chamber. Liquid materials in the very short time of the combustion cycle appear solid because of their mass and simply give the combustion chamber the effect of having a 'tight chamber. In other words, you may show signs of over pressure because you have carried liquid into the chamber and that liquid is not compressible during the firing cycle, therefore pressures go up. You see this sometimes when you are shooting in the rain and you track water into the chamber along with the ammo. You will sometimes see signs of over pressure simply because the water is not compressible.

Q. At what point is the green or blue on the patches, from the jag or brush, and not from the bullet residue?
Charlie: "When you stop using the brass, copper or bronze jag/brush it can only come from the jacket fouling. Use a plastic or aluminum slotted tip when *wet patching*."

Boots: "Color is a precipitant - Not the actual material, small amounts in cracks will cause color long after bore is clean."

Q. Clean hot (right after shooting) or does it matter?
Jim: "After eating a spaghetti dinner, if you rinse the plate right away, it is ninety percent clean with little or no effort. Let it set for a couple of hours and dry, the cleaning job becomes far greater and requires more scrubbing."

Charlie: "Yes - barrel is warm and expanded and the chemical reaction is accelerated."

Boots: "When warm is a little better."

Q. So what is the real deal on Sweet's 7.62 solvent?
Charlie: "IT WORKS! - But remove after 15 minutes. OK to re-coat for further cleaning. After cleaning with Sweets, dry the bore, then wet the bore with Hoppes #9 to dilute and neutralize the stronger cleaner and to protect the bore with rust inhibitors found in Hoppes #9."

Q. With the new Moly bullet coatings, is there any change to the routine for cleaning? Is cleaning still necessary? Does it reduce fouling as advertised?
Charlie: "First impression—good stuff—less fouling, big reduction in cleaning. Theory: probable increase in bore life."

Boots: "Doesn't eliminate all fouling, but reduces frequency of the need to clean from reports."

Q. Does Cryogenic Treatment reduce fouling and improve accuracy as advertised?
Boots: "Cryogenic Treatment causes an alignment of atomic structure - reduces harmonic side notes 'WE THINK.' Alignment appears to reduce spalling of bore so should reduce fouling - but not a 100% change - it's a hedge."

Q. So how come barrels aren't all frozen now if it is that good?
Charlie: "$$$$$$$$ and some people live and shoot in warm places like Florida, Hawaii, Arizona, etc. and I'm afraid they might melt."

Boots: "Cost! Gain is more like 15 to 20% on target barrels at MAX., maybe zero. Not of cost value for average hunter. Cryo will increase machinability—that may mean a better fit and chamber job."

Jim: Jack says it makes the barrels easier for the barrel maker to work on.

Q. Is Break Free still the best for lubing?
Charlie: "I still use it and like it but I don't have the time for testing the numerous new products out there. Ml's and M-14's need grease."

Q. When do you use Quick Scrub?
No one answered this one except Jon Wilcox: "Almost never - only to clean an AR-15 gas tube."

Q. At what number on the erosion gauge does the rifle generally lose accuracy?
Charlie: "Depends on the load, the rifle, the bullet and the cartridge OAL."

Boots: "Rifling systems vary, my deep rifled barrels shoot much longer. Erosion gauge is only relative to bore design it was developed for. Usually 4gr 300X308."

Q. So how come barrels aren't all micro polished and surface treated etc.?
Charlie: "$$$$$$$$ and sometimes these processes are used only in an attempt to salvage barrels not made right in the first

place. Add the cost of doing this to a less than premium grade barrel and what have you got? A more expensive barrel that still might not be satisfactory in the long run. Invest in a premium grade barrel in the first place and you'll KNOW it will shoot well."

Boots: "Many claims are gimmicks. One maker kept end of barrel that was electro polished to compare before and after, the before came out better than the after. It's quality workmanship that makes a good barrel."

Q. I know Hoppe's bore cleaner is one of the most popular bore cleaners, but what about old (WW2 or Korean era) GI bore cleaner? Is it as good as current day cleaners? Does it go bad? Should it be mixed with another cleaner? There is a lot of it on the market, and it sells pretty cheap.
Charlie: "Good question - I don't have the answer."

Boots: "Some old GI cleaners were water soluble to remove corrosive primer residue, not compatible with current ammo."

Q. What are the pros and cons of M-14 rifle barrels: 6 - groove 1/10, 6 - groove 1/12, 6 groove 1/11, 4 groove 1/10, as it relates to 100, 200, 300 & 600 yards and 168 gr. or 173 gr. bullets? Information on the above as relates to the H-bar would not hurt.
Charlie: "My experience has been 6 groove barrels in general have not exhibited the accuracy of the 4 groove barrels with the 173 Gr. bullet. The 168 gr. is a tossup between the 4 or 6 depending on the individual barrel. When in doubt about twist rate—err on the fast side. Over stabilization has marginal affects on accuracy—under stabilization can create flyers (gross inaccuracy). A ten twist will stabilize a heavier bullet better than a twelve twist etc. Stay within the accepted range of the industry for the best results."

Boots: "4 groove was used to develop the GI 173 gr. With a hard jacket. The bullet doesn't generally function well in the 6 groove barrels, plus many 6 groove barrels are button rifled and shallow with 302-303 bores. It's the lands that do the work—NOT THE GROOVE. 5R and deep bores so far has been the best with 298x308 5R's lasting 6 - 9,000 rds. It also beat out everything else in 'Life vs Accuracy' government test for sniper barrels in the 80's on the old 300X308 bore. In 1996 cut rifled 298X308 5R's showed up best in Fort Bragg Special Forces testing of SR-25's. If in doubt, use a one in eleven twist, it will shoot all regular bullets."

Q. In choosing a barrel for a service rifle there are two materials available - stainless steel and chrome moly. My M1A barrel is nearing the end of its lifetime so I'm looking for a replacement. I've always assumed I'd get a stainless Krieger barrel since the longer life means fewer barrels down the line. However, my gunsmith recommends that I get a chrome moly barrel. He contends that the relatively rough bore in a stainless barrel must be lapped by bullets during firing and the extended life of the stainless barrel is mostly shortened by the time the barrel has to be shot before reaching comparable performance with a chrome moly barrel*. He has even seen jackets torn off bullets** in new stainless barrels which won't happen with chrome moly. What do Obermeyer and Krieger have to say?

Charlie: * "Must NOT have been an Obermeyer or Krieger barrel - probably a button rifle barrel." ** "Jackets torn off of bullets?? Bullets can shed jackets for a number of reasons, some of which are; 1) too fast a twist rate for the construction of the bullet. It literally flies apart from centrifugal force. 2) Too thin a jacket, as above plus deep rifling or a sharp rifling profile can induce stress points in the jacket, which will weaken it, causing failure. 3) Too high a velocity for the bullet —centrifugal force again. A Bore rough enough to TEAR the jacket off a bullet - would probably, hopefully and most likely visually prevent you from using it. Pushing a patch through it and checking the remains of that patch, if any exits, would definitely tell the story."

Boots: "Stainless steel actually wears faster but throat stays smoother hence less vertical stringing at long ranges, this is more of a plus on a bolt rifle due to heavy bullets and loads. Stainless steel won't throat harden so that it can be set back, giving longer life to the barrel. For bolt target rifles stainless steel is ahead due to set back and verticals. On M-14 & M-l's Chrome Moly may reduce problems with peaning and cleaning rod wear. You can't set back with CM. Loads are usually medium wt. and milder. I say it's 50/50 on gas guns. It will outlast SS for life for usable battle field accuracy."

Q. To brush or not to brush? There is a continuing debate in our club whether or not to use a bore brush in quality match barrels. Many claim that just patches will remove the fouling from a good quality barrel and that bore brushes can introduce micro-scratches, particularly in stainless barrels. I have found that my Douglas barrel definitely needs brushing to remove all the fouling and I wonder what I should consider with a new barrel?
Charlie: "Patches & solvents - brushing only to hurry things along when you don't have the time to let the solvent do the work - then use the phosphor bronze only and brush very carefully."

Q. So where do the gunsmiths buy those storage lockers. You know, the ones where they put your rifle for a year before they begin to work on it?
Charlie: "I want to know too. I just throw them in a pile and pull out the bottom one to work on. Keeps them in order you know."

Boots: "A YEAR...Who works that fast?"

Bolt Guns

Q. Is it OK to lube the bolt lugs with a Teflon based oil?
Charlie: "Why not?"

Boots: "I use synthetic wheel bearing grease, it won't run in heat."

M-1A

Q. I have had people tell me I should NEVER remove the receiver from the stock - not even once a year for cleaning due to the chance of damaging the glass bedding. What do you gentlemen recommend?

Charlie: "Carefully take it apart annually. You have to disassemble the rifle to thoroughly clean the op-rod & its related parts and inspect the receiver and the bedding. You might be surprised how much lube etc. is between the receiver & the bedding. Only by carefully dismantling, cleaning, visually inspecting and lubing the individual parts and sub-assembles of the rifle, can you prevent damage or the furthering of damage. This is the goal of maintenance. To keep the rifle operating properly (accurately) as long as possible without the necessity of replacing parts at great expense. Minor adjustments can be made at low cost which will likely prevent catastrophic failure (which always occurs at the worst possible time). When your rifle fails in the middle of a leg match, you will know the benefit of preventive maintenance."

Q. How often should I completely breakdown my M-14 for cleaning?

Charlie: "Annually or as needed. But no more than absolutely necessary."

Q. What are the tell-tail signs of your glass bedding breaking down?

Charlie: "Looseness of the receiver in the stock - crumbling, cracking of the bedding compound. Do not confuse easy removal of receiver with bad bedding, Some receivers have a slight taper which allows them to remove easily."

Mike: "The groups get larger rather quickly. That seems to be an indicator."

Q. I store my M-1A muzzle down in my gun vault to prevent cleaning solvents from getting to the glass bedding. A friend told me the rifle should not rest on the flash suppressor. What is your opinion on this? If it is not a

Care, Cleaning & Sportsmanship

good idea to store muzzle down resting on the flash suppressor - how would you do it in a gun vault?
Charlie: "It won't hurt the flash suppressor, if you don't drop it on the suppressor. Make sure the suppressor is not plugged before firing. You can make a small bracket

And hang the rifle upside down using the rear sling swivel. But if it breaks, the rifle will fall and land on the flash suppressor. NEVER tempt Murphy!!"

Mike: "The flash suppressor will take the weight of the rifle as long as you don't bang it around. Storing with the muzzle down will help with preventing the solvents from flowing into the glass bedding. A patch on the closed bolt will also help. The AR-15 has a synthetic stock (no glass bedding) and the solvents are not a problem."

Q. How does one clean out the gas system & how often should it be done?
Charlie: "For the M-14, see the text of Chapter Three."

Mike: "For the AR-15 the gas tube is self cleaning. I have had only two instances where it had to be cleaned, other than a piece of patch getting stuck in the gas port while trying to clean the barrel. One instance was someone using military surplus powder with a lot of flash suppressant, probably too slow a powder for the application, it produced a lot of goo that gummed up everything including the gas tube. The other was a customer who thought that small PISTOL primers were as good as small rifle primers. He was getting such poor ignition that a lot of residue was getting caught in the gas tube. Other than that, the gas flows from the port to the rear and is generally self cleaning with good commercial powders and the proper burn rate. If you do need to clean the gas tube you can use some carburetor cleaner which is predominantly Toluene, a good solvent. You can use an aerosol can with a spray nozzle extension to spray the cleaner into the gas tube, which is visible inside the upper receiver. The bolt and carrier will be removed and when you look down the bore from the breech to the muzzle you can see the carb cleaner enter the barrel as you spray it down the gas tube. A little bit of cleaner will certainly take out anything that's inside the tube. You then should blow it out with compressed air. Make sure to oil the bore, the Toluene will take out any rust inhibitors."

Jon Wilcox: "I wrap an Industrial paper towel patch around the brush and use a Hoppes T-Handle. I can cut 9/ sheet - much less costly than patches & tough too."

Q. I use the ratchet type breech brush to clean the breech of my M-14, I usually wrap it with a cleaning patch and saturate it with Hoppe's to clean the breech. Should I use this process or should I use it without the patch and only use the bristle to clean the breech.
Charlie: "Use the patch - pinch the patch on the brush; got poked huh - the bristles still do the work, the patch soaks up and carries away the crud."

Mike: "When I use the AR-15 chamber brush I make a handle out of a couple of sections of a steel cleaning rod. Screw one into the brush and bend the second section into an "L" to form a handle. I use the brush without a patch on it, just make sure the brush is WET, Hoppes works great. You want it wet to flush any particulate matter away from the chamber. The brush won't harm the chamber but the particulate matter could be abrasive enough to do it some damage. As with anything I place in the breech or bore use it wet to keep from grinding in all the stuff you are supposed to be taking out."

Q. Best way to clean the bore of M-1A?
Charlie: "Carefully "VERY" carefully." See text.

Q. Normally I only clean the bore and breech. What about the bolt and trigger group?
Charlie: "Bolt very often neglected - especially the face & extractor. Trigger group as needed - Requires dismantling - which will relieve bedding tension on conventional bedded M-14's. No problem on lugged rifles."

Q. Best bullet recipe for 1,000 yards and is this rifle competitive (Service Rifle class)?
Jim: "The Marine Corps and the Army use the M-14 at 1,000 yds. All the time."

Care, Cleaning & Sportsmanship

Boots: "Try the Sierra 175 gr."

Q. So why do people think that 200 grain bullets are hard on the gas system when I have proved that they are gentler than the 168's and 150's. Don't believe me? Give me a call at (803)-284-4909)
Boots: "It's not the bullet, it's the pressure on the gas port - 12,000 cup (copper unit pressure) for an M-14. Too much pressure and you hammer the bolt back into the rear of the receiver."

Q. What is the real figure for gas port pressure? C. E. Harris sez the gas port works on 9K + or - 2K. But the pressure at 14 inches down the tube is about 17 to 19K according to sure articles. And how is the pressure at 6K at 23.5 inches in the .308 M-1 if it is 9K at 14 in the M-1A? You'll probably need an Oehler 43 and some time at the range for this one.
Charlie: "Different powder, primer, and bullet weights and profiles will create these differences. Bore pressure decreases as distance from the chamber increases."

Boots: "M-16 port pressure is 16,500 plus or minus 2,000. You need to be on the plus side to work or function well."

Q. Does indexing the cases for slow fire at 600 and 1,000 yards have any effect for the Service Rifle? Is it time well spent?
Charlie: "Easier to use cartridges with minimum run out* than to index, too much fiddling."

  * See: *Sight Alignment, Trigger Control and The Big Lie*, page 84.

Mike: "The point of case indexing is basically to correct a problem that may exist if the chamber is not cut on the center line of the bore. There might be deformation of the case and indexing would re-align it. If you are so unfortunate to have an AR-15 with a chamber that is not on the same center line as the bore, you might find indexing might help. The multiple lugs of the AR-15 give a more uniform lock up and the bullet does not have a stiff direction and a flexible direction as the two lug lock up on the M-1 and M1A."

Boots: "Mostly B.S., haven't found gain worthwhile - mostly in peoples' heads. Most people blame little things on their ammo, giving them a scapegoat to blame, they need to hold better."

Q. How do YOU anneal your cases?
Charlie: "I never use them that long in a gas gun."

Boots: "I stand them in a pan of water about 1/2 submerged, then heat the necks with a torch until they just start to turn red. I don't knock them over, I just let them cool."

Q. Is there a preferred light load at 200 yards which functions well? (Such as the 39 grains of 4064 that Tubb likes.)
Charlie: "The most accurate one in your rifle."

Boots: "In my bolt gun I use 42 gr. of Reloader 15 with the 168 gr. Sierra bullet. IMR was about 41 gr. but quality of powder is ???"

Q. Can you shoot moly coated bullets in the rapids without fear of a small misalignment during feeding sinking a bullet in the case, and causing pressures to skyrocket? Is there a problem mixing moly and non-moly for the different stages in order to preclude this fear?
Jim: "See Chapter Four"

Q. Is there an outfit which makes inserts for the hooded rear aperture so that you can reduce the opening from .0520 for a better F-stop? Jones makes lenses which go in the sight so maybe someone is making aperture inserts.
Jim: "Mike Bykowski of High Performance International (414-466-9040) is currently making an interchangeable hooded rear aperture for the AR-15 that will not change your zero when you switch from one to the other.

Q. Who specializes in Service Rifle sights?—Mine seem a bit wobbly.
Jim: Northern Compaction, has excellent AR-15 sights, 1/4 Min. windage and elevation. Call Lee at 262-498-3897.

Care, Cleaning & Sportsmanship

Q. Where can you get decent barrels for the Service Rifle in 7-08, 6.5-08 etc.?

Mike: "This is kind of a funny question because neither of those are calibers that a service rifle can be shot, if you consider the "service rifle" a rifle defined by the service rifle rules, there is no such thing as a service rifle 7-08 or 6.5-08. If you mean an M-1, M1A or AR-15 in a non-service rifle configuration, then Krieger Barrels or Obermeyer Rifled Barrels are your best source to get high quality bores & twist in service rifle type barrels.

Boots: "Can be made, have done 7X08 but life drops - Is it worthwhile? Not a Service Rifle."

M-1

Q. How do you clean the channel by the gas port?

Charlie: "Pipe cleaner and solvent. Be careful, pipe cleaners have a wire it them which can put scratches in the bore wall opposite the port."

AR-15

Q. Do the multi lugs negate the need for case indexing?

Charlie: "Same as above, Easier to use cartridges with minimum run out* than to index, too much fiddling."

* Again see: *Sight Alignment, Trigger Control and The Big Lie*, page 84.

Mike: "Actually No, if the upper and lower receiver are slightly loose it doesn't affect accuracy. You do get accuracy problems when they are too tight. When they are too tight it means you are twisting one with respect to the other to get the pins to go in. The upper receiver on an AR is not a stress part, it is a thin shelled aluminum forging. It carries the rear sight, so if you twist it to make it match up with the pins you will have problems that will effect accuracy as that twist works back and forth. The problem occurs when the rattle is so loud it starts to work on your head and you start to think about it. It could affect your shooting, even though it doesn't affect the mechanical system. You can put a little polyurethane plug, called an 'Accu-wedge' between the lower receiver and the rear lug of the upper receiver, that takes the rattle out so you don't have to think about it, yet it doesn't over stress the upper receiver."

Q. What are the good loads for the AR?

Jim: "Varget powder and Gold Medal Federal Match Primers is a match made in heaven. I loaded 25.3 gr. of Varget powder with 69 gr. Sierra bullets, Mag. length, and shot a ten shot group at 200 yards (bench rested & scope). The group was the size of the tip of your thumb and the first joint. I loaded 24.0 grs of Varget powder and 80 gr. Sierra bullets and tested groups at 200 yds (bench rested & scope) using the Stony Point OAL gage and the Bullet Comparator. I found the overall length of my chamber and made up loads (ten rounds each) set .005, .010, .015, .020, .025, .030, .035 and .040 thousandths deeper. My rifle liked the one set .010 off the lands. The size of the group? Nine out of ten touched a One-Half inch circle at 200 yards, the tenth shot was just off. I write the data on a plain white sheet of paper with a three quarter inch black paster in the center and tape it to the target. I'm not trying to hit the paster, just shoot group sizes. I then use a MR-52 target (600 yd. reduced for 200 yds) copied on a transparency ($.50 at Kinko's (*now called FedEx Office in most areas*)) as an overlay. Both groups made a score of 100 with ten X's.

Mike: "It's too much to go into here. My plans are to ask people who shoot good scores and keep good data to write down their pet loads and share them with other customers. Bullets: 69 gr. Sierra was the first of the high quality bullets and is still used a good deal at 200 & 300 yards. The 75 gr. Hornady has the best external ballistics of any bullet that can be shot out of the magazine, and it can be shot at 200, 300 and 600 yards. The 80 gr. Sierra is probably the current favorite for 600 yds. And beyond shooting in .22 cal. Hornady is developing a new 75 gr. bullet with a long plastic nose that will have a better ballistic coefficient than the 80 gr. Sierra. If it groups, the production run should have begun by the time you read this. It will give the 80 gr. Sierra a run for its money. As far as powders go, the current favorite is the VihtaVuori Oy N-135 for the 68, 69, 70 gr. groupings up to the 75 gr. bullet; N-140 is a good powder for the 70, 75, 80 gr. bullets. N-540 the new High Energy powder is what the Army is using in both their 69 gr. Sierra and 80 gr. Sierra loads. Varget is a good powder that is used in both the 69 gr. and 80 gr. Sierra loads. For the cases I mostly use Lake City military cases. I have tried some Federal cases and have not been thrilled with the results; the metal is very soft and the primer pockets open up rather quickly, the brass is somewhat fragile. For commercial brass Winchester is quite good and so is IMI brass. Primers: my favorite is the Federal Match primers, some people swear by Winchester Match primers which are also very good."

Q. When is Sierra and Hornady going to discount their .308 bullets now that everyone is buying .22's?

Jim: "Right after they find that pig in the back hills of Tennessee that really can whistle."

Charlie: "When the last grunt leaves the firing line."

Boots: "When Clinton tells the Truth."

Mike: "I'm really afraid that .308 bullets are going to get more expensive. Everyone is shooting .22 cal. and no one's buying .308 cal. As you know, when production volume goes down the unit price gets more expensive to produce. So I would expect .308 bullet prices would go up just like the .50 cal. bullets did."

Q. This one is not so much a question but do you have any comments?

Jim: I have been gunsmithing for about 35 years and work on all the service rifles and build bolt action match and varmint rifles. I have been working on the AR-15s for about two years and have had some good results. I shoot high power and switched to the AR year before last. The rifle I am shooting has a Krieger CM barrel and only been used with Moly coated

bullets, cleaning has been from the breech using a rod guide and Shooters Choice MC-7 bore cleaner. I find that 4 or 5 wet patches does the job, I run a brush through once in a while just to see if anything will come out. I clean the chamber with a Hoppe's nylon chamber brush with a patch wrapped around it and MC-7 followed by a dry patch. I clean the bolt and carrier with Hoppes #9 or the MC-7 to remove carbon and remove the carbon from inside the carrier with the solvent and careful scraping. Lubrication on the outside of the carrier is Kleen Bore TW-25B grease applied in small amounts and rubbed in. I also use a small amount of Shooters Choice FP-10 on the rear of the bolt and inside the carrier where the bolt is placed, I think this helps to keep the carbon soft. This procedure is followed each time the rifle is fired. The only malfunction I have had is the rifle has doubled on one occasion. My question would be what causes this?* the rifle has a Milazzo trigger which was set at 4.75 lbs at the time of the problem and all loads were checked for high primers. I know you did not ask for my experience, but I thought you may find it helpful when you get going with the book.
   - Sincerely, Bob Lovett USMC 1957-60

Charlie: * "Probable cause; insufficient over travel - caused by improper installation, not enough over travel, loctite wedging the disconnector, piece of debris found its way into the action. Contact me."

Mike: "With the Milazzo trigger properly installed it is impossible to double without something breaking.

There are some things that appear to be doubles; if you kind of 'Ride' the trigger it is possible to fire two shots in rapid succession. While two shots fired, it is not an uncontrolled double. It's possible there is something wrong with the installation of the Milazzo trigger. I was thinking if I ever heard of an AR-15 so called 'Slam Firing,' and I have not. The only time I've seen it happen, the force of the carrier going home actually knocked the hammer off the trigger because the trigger had an improper trigger job on it. Improperly reworked standard triggers can double because there is a very critical relationship on the disconnector and most novices in attempting to stone and rework it don't get it right and it's much easier to get it wrong than it is to get it right. Trigger jobs on standard parts evolve reshaping, rehardening and then refitting in a very specific order. It's relatively complicated and shouldn't be tried by an amateur gunsmith."

Comments

Charlie: "Accuracy equals = Properly built & maintained rifle + properly equipped shooter + properly constructed ammunition + concentration (and a whole lot a luck doesn't hurt either)."

Boots: "Put all B.S. aside and PRACTICE!"

CHAPTER SIX

Cleaning, Lubricating, Maintenance & Storage of Firearms

By Rick Jerry

Let's start out this topic by giving the warning, NEVER STORE YOUR FIREARM IN A CASE! Gun cases are designed for the legal transportation of firearms, not storage. Either a hard case or a soft one will, manufacturers' claims notwithstanding, attract, trap and hold moisture. This causes and/or accelerates **RUSTING!**

A lot of gun owners have the best of intentions regarding getting to the task of proper cleaning and maintenance, but are in some cases, a bit forgetful. When you bring your firearm home from the range or hunting, bring it INSIDE, and REMOVE IT from the case. The change in temperature and/or humidity especially in the fall and winter causes condensation to form on the entire firearm when "brought in from the cold" (People who wear eyeglasses can relate to this). When left in the case, the condensation is trapped in contact with the parts of the firearm. If left unattended, this causes rusting of the ferrous metal parts. It makes no difference whether the case has a cloth or foam lining, RUSTING will occur in either. We have seen extreme incidents where the case actually bonded itself to the metal! It takes only a couple of minutes of attention to prevent costly damage to your firearm.

Know your cleaners, lubricants, and solvents.

Did you know, for example, that WD-40® has a fish-oil base, that when the carrier agent evaporates off, leaves a sticky coating that, when it dries has a stronger bonding effect than some of the varieties of Loc-Tite®? There are actually some industrial applications in which WD-40® is used as a locking agent, instead of Loc-Tite®! What does that say about its lubricating properties?

Tri-Flo® or Tri-Flon®, in addition to having a Teflon content, has a carrying agent that attracts and bonds with dirt and grit, forming a very aggressive abrasive. It has recently been determined that Break-Free (CLP) ® as used extensively by the military, also has a long-term degenerative quality (gumming). It is being replaced in elite units such as the U.S. Navy Seals by a newer product sold under the trade name of Firepower FP-10® Lubricant Elite. It is NOT the same formula sold by Venco as Shooter's Choice FP-10®. (The Shooter's Choice variant has only the lubrication portion of the original formula). The product sold in the white containers bearing the name FIREPOWER FP-10® is the same product used by the Seals, FBI, and many other federal agencies and military units. It comes highly recommended!

Solvents are another matter. There are millions of people who still swear by (or at) Hoppe's No. 9®. Fine. The EPA recently made the Frank A. Hoppe Davison of Penguin Industries remove the Benzene from the formula for No. 9, fearing that infants or children might suffer from proximity inhalation of the benzene fumes. Do you clean your firearms in the nursery?! Not nearly as many people still drive Model T Fords. Why? Newer and better products evolve. It's called progress. While either Hoppe's No. 9® or a Model T still do the job, better, faster and more efficient ways have been found to accomplish their given tasks, which makes life a lot easier and more enjoyable. While Hoppe's now markets a product they call Benchrest No. 9 Copper Solvent®, it works slowly and incompletely. It's kind of like moving up to a Model A Ford from your Model T.

Among the most modern, effective solvents, is a product from Venco called Shooter's Choice MC#7® Bore Solvent. It's fast, simple and effective. Following label directions will take care of the job efficiently. If you happen to have an older rifle that's starting to lose its accuracy, and just normal cleaning doesn't seem to help, follow a cleaning with Shooter's Choice with an application of Shooter's Choice Copper Solvent®. The two products are 100% compatible.

Among other very effective copper solvents are Barnes (as in Barnes Bullets) CR-10®. It is among the fastest and easiest to use. Another brand is called Pro-Shot Copper Solvent II®. My personal choice is the Barnes CR-10®. It doesn't foam and is non-corrosive.

DO NOT MIX BRANDS OF SOLVENTS AND COPPER SOLVENTS! A corrosive chemical reaction may occur, causing barrel damage! Cleaning a bore exclusively with only a copper solvent is both counter-productive and a bit expensive. If you're going to do the job, at least take the time and make the effort to do it correctly.

NEVER USE A SOFT OR JOINTED CLEANING ROD!

A multiple piece and/or soft (brass, aluminum or wood rod), or, for that matter, a soft (or even stainless) steel one-piece cleaning rod can do more harm than good! Barrel fouling can become imbedded in the material and/or joints of the rod and act as an abrasive, damaging your barrel. It's the equivalent of using a radial file as a cleaning rod substitute! The rod of choice is a one-piece, coated (with a synthetic material), of the proper length and diameter for your particular barrel. It is recommended that the rod be wiped down at the end of each stroke, so as to remove any potentially dangerous "grit" that it may have picked up in its travels. The reason for using the rod closest to the bore diameter is twofold: first, it reduces "rod flex" which can, over time, wear out the rifling, and second, it reduces the possibility of damage or bending to the rod itself. The rods of choice are either the Dewey one-piece coated rods, or the same type by Parker-Hale.

NEVER USE A STAINLESS STEEL BORE BRUSH

Stainless steel bore brushes have destroyed more barrels than any other type! Unless you have a major problem, a synthetic brush should be used. Brass and "phosphor bronze" brushes are susceptible to damage by the more aggressive of the new breed of bore solvents. If the solvents can remove copper (jacket) fouling, they can also "eat" brass and bronze brushes.

USE COTTON FLANNEL PATCHES

Cotton flannel or "Duck" patches do a more thorough job of carrying solvents and lubricants, as well as removing fouling, than do the newer synthetic (Remie) patches sold by Outers and some other manufacturers. If your patches are a bright white color and the fibers all seem to run the same direction, you probably have the synthetic variety. Ox-Yoke G.I. patches are of "Cotton."

WHENEVER POSSIBLE, CLEAN YOUR FIREARMS "SIGHTS-DOWN"

Cleaning your firearm in the "sights-down" or inverted position prevents liquids and fluids from seeping and migrating into the bedding or the stock. A device such as a Decker Rifle Vise or an MTM Rifle Maintenance Center is a convenient way to position a long gun in the inverted position so as to minimize this problem.

USE A "ROD GUIDE"

Whether you clean from the breech (bolt end), by far the preferred method, or from the muzzle (which may be necessitated by your firearm's action type), always use a rod guide. They serve several purposes. The most important is to help prevent damage to the rifling caused by a "sharp" corner of rod striking either the "lead" or origin of the rifling, or, even worse, nicking the crown of the barrel, the part that the bullet "sees" last upon exiting the barrel. Of secondary importance is the ability of a properly fitting rod guide to minimize the seepage of solvents and lubricants into places they don't belong, such as your trigger group or gas system.

CLEAN MORE THAN JUST THE BARREL BORE

Of the people who claim to have judiciously cleaned their firearm(s), the greatest percentage cleaned only the interior of the barrel (bore). While you may get away with this practice for awhile, the neglect of the firearm will eventually take its toll. Gas operated firearms are especially unforgiving of such neglect. In gas operated firearms, it is essential to clean the chamber each time you clean the bore. Most military, ex-military, military look-alikes and some commercial "gas guns" have a dedicated chamber brush that was especially designed for them. Get one and use it. There are similar commercial products made to clean the bolt raceways and locking lugs of most bolt action rifles. A very handy item for getting into those hard to reach areas that seem to really like to attract and harbor "grunge" is the surgical swab. It is essentially a single-ended "Q-Tip" on a 6-inch wooden stick. You can use it either dry or saturated with your favorite solvent to get the carbon, etc. out of those hard to reach places. Not doing so leaves an abrasive paste that accelerates the wear of close fitting moving parts.

Jim Owens

GAS SYSTEMS

Since there is little similarity between the gas systems of various makes and models of gas operated firearms, I'm going to be quite general in my treatment of them. Bluntly put, if your action is misbehaving and the symptoms are getting worse, then it is time to diagnose the problem(s). Most of these problems are related to neglect of the gas system. Up until 1986, the U.S. military taught complete disassembly and cleaning of firearms after each day's use. At about this time it occurred to someone that all that disassembly and reassembly was causing unnecessary wear to the parts involved, actually causing more harm than good. Someone in the "think-tank" came to the realization that henceforth one should only do a complete tear-down when a problem occurred, or at the end of a cycle (such as the competitive shooting year), whichever came first. It works!

Shooters of M-14s and/or the commercial equivalent

Springfield Army M1A® are taught to routinely elevate then lower the muzzle of their rifles with the action open, and listen for the gas piston to travel and bottom out. You can hear it move. If it doesn't, or moves slower than normal, it's time to clean the gas system. In the M-14/M1A there are some special tools made for getting the carbon buildup out of the gas piston and the gas cylinder plug. It is not unusual for these rifles to change point of impact on a target due to the carbon buildup in these parts. It may seem insignificant to you, but it can mean the difference between a winning and a losing score, or in a military application, life or death (The M-14 is still the rifle of choice of the U.S. Navy Seals, naval mine snipers assigned to mine sweepers, and several other military and government agencies). By the way, keep the gas piston and cylinder dry. If they are wet, they accelerate the fouling process.

BOLTS, ETC.

It is essential to keep the working parts of a bolt clean. This includes, but is not limited to, the bolt face and extractor recesses. A buildup of debris, either carbon or brass, can have an adverse effect on performance and reliability. The surgical swab comes in handy here, too.

THE DREADED KILLER FLASH HIDER/ MUZZLE BRAKE

Flash hider/suppressors and/or muzzle brakes serve many purposes. They do, however, require care and cleaning. Carbon deposits build up in all of them to varying extents, be they on handguns or long guns, and that affects accuracy. My first experience with this problem was on an old High Standard Supermatic Trophy 7 112 .22 L.R. target pistol. The combination of lead, paraffin and carbon build up had almost completely clogged the slots in the brake. It doesn't take the proverbial rocket scientist to figure out that the tool included with the muzzle brake was intended to serve as a cleaning tool as well. The flash hiders on military rifles and their civilian look-alikes also collect carbon which, if left unattended, degrades the accuracy of the rifle. Cleaning brushes of approximately .45 cal. and patches and swabs saturated with solvent will do the job of cleaning these problem areas. When no more fouling appears, dry the affected areas thoroughly, but do not lubricate! Lubrication of either the gas system parts or flash hider/muzzle brake surfaces is self-defeating, as it only intensifies the problem by attracting and holding future carbon. These recommendations apply to the "BOSS®" system and its copies, and Magna-Porting, as well.

SIGHTS NEED ATTENTION, TOO

For those of us who use calcium carbide "smokers" or lamps to "blacken" our sights and, in some cases, portions of our barrels, it is easy to forget to remove the carbide residue. This can be a costly mistake. The carbide is hygroscopic; that is to say, it attracts and holds moisture in contact with the parts to which it has been applied. In other words, carbide is a "rust magnet!" Several persons to whom I have pointed out this fact have come back to me in amazement after having removed carbide to find major rust underneath.

The moving parts of adjustable sights require proper lubrication. The functional recommendation here is: Moderation! On a service rifle, the gears and pinions should be lightly greased with an all-weather grease. I have used Shooter's Choice High Tech Gun Grease® and high temperature bearing grease with equal effectiveness. Under no circumstances get any type of grease or lube on the actual sight aperture! It is like looking through a soap bubble, complete with color aberrations.

MORE IS NOT NECESSARILY BETTER

There are those who believe that if a little of something is good, then more must logically be better. Not so! The use of excessive amounts of any fluids in cleaning or preservation can be harmful. A light coating is far superior to a heavy one. If you like "more," "check your oil" occasionally and add another light coating, but only if needed.

PROTECT YOUR STOCK, NOT JUST THE METAL PARTS

Stocks, especially wood stocks require extra care. The single worst thing you can do to a firearm with a wood stock is to store it in a safe, rack or closet with the muzzle POINTING UP and the butt pointed down! It really makes no viable difference how many coats of what kind of "Wonder Finish" the wood may have on it, the fluids you used to clean and/or preserve the metal are going to follow Newton's Law of gravity, and migrate down into the stock where they attack the cellulose fibers. Many older long guns are visibly darker in the wrist or pistol grip area of the stock from long years of upright storage and the effects of fluid migration. No finish on the wood at all makes matters worse, as moisture from the air causes expansion and contraction of the wood, and thus weakens it. Anyone who has ever had the displeasure of having to shoot in the rain for any amount of time knows just how bad the effects can be on point-of-impact, caused by the moisture swelling the wood fibers and changing bedding pressure.

The highly reflective finish on many Remington stocks is a Du Pont synthetic bowling pin finish called RKW. It may not be aesthetically pleasing, but it is very effective in sealing the wood. It is almost impossible to remove without damaging the wood underneath. If you are a "do-it-yourselfer" when it comes to finishing gun stocks, finish them with a high quality polyurethane finish. It is available in flat, semi-gloss and glossy to suit your style. Be sure to use at least five coats, allowing them to dry thoroughly and wet-sanding them between coats. Make sure you cover all of the exposed wood of the stock, not just the exterior. Be certain to get the base of the stock, as well as any cavities or traps. Any unfinished exposed cellulose is a moisture magnet.

FORGO THE SHORTCUTS

We all know that it's human nature to look for the easy way out. Remember what P.T. Barnum once said about there being "a sucker born every minute . . . ." There are all kinds of gadgets out there that we just can't seem to do without, even if they really don't make things easier. Some huckster will make us think they can save us time, or whatever.

Proper maintenance of a firearm requires the same things it did a hundred or more years ago. Recall when you were in the service and your D.I. got on your case: concentration and "elbow grease." There are those who would prey on your feelings, those with sonic baths and electronic "doodads." Resist the temptation. I know of one poor sinner who couldn't resist, and totally ruined the chrome lined barrels on THREE M-1 Garands, two M1As and an AR-15 by using the dreaded "foul-o-matic." The concept is appealing: since fouling is nothing more than a metal plating of the bore, why not use reverse electroplating? Chrome lined bores are why not!

MICRO-BREWING (OR CAN I BUILD A BETTER MOUSETRAP)

With the cost of an uninstalled quality rifle barrel running from $200 to $500+, do you really think that you can come up with your own "secret formula" for a bore cleaner or copper solvent and not have to "pay the piper?" Do you have a Doctorate in Chemical Engineering and a fully equipped and funded research lab? My brother-in law does, and he hasn't had the urge to improve on the wheel. On the other end of the spectrum, I know a welder who thought he knew better. The welder concocted a home-brew consisting of a type of industrial ammonia, Slick-50®, and a few other odds and ends he happened to have lying around. He could have sold the stuff to Saddam Hussein as a chemical warfare agent, because you couldn't stand to be downwind of the guy when he uncorked the stuff. It actually ate the brass fittings off of several cleaning rods. Imagine what it did to his barrels! After ruining several hundred dollars worth of barrels, he got a couple swift kicks and a dose of mental health, and is now using commercial solvents. By the way, the brother-in law developed a chemical for extracting the last little bits of copper from its bore for one of the major mining companies out in Montana. He promised to send me some, but it's just as well he didn't. It seems that one of the "short-cutters" on the cleanup crew at the plant decided to use "live" steam to speed up the cleaning of the vat in which the stuff had been made. The stench was so bad that they had to evacuate a five mile radius around the plant! And you thought your "significant other" disliked the smell of the commercial solvent you're using! Janell loves the smell of Hoppes #9®!

Care, Cleaning & Sportsmanship

TO EPA OR NOT TO EPA, IS THAT A QUESTION?

There may be one short cut I may unofficially endorse. Aerosol cans (no CFCs) of automotive brake cleaner. DO NOT SUBSTITUTE CARBURETOR CLEANER OR FUEL INJECTOR CLEANER! You can use it to flush out trigger mechanisms, gas systems, degrease just about anything, and it even gets a lot of carbon out. It comes in handy for rinsing out a few things, like bore brushes and service rifle sights (gets the carbide off). Whatever you use it on will need almost immediate re-lubrication, but it does flush out a lot of garbage, especially in hard to get at areas like service rifle bolts and semi-auto pistol actions (for which I learned about it, at the Sheriff's department.)

THINGS NOT TO DO

Don't use your pressure washer on your firearms. Don't dip your ammunition in Teflon®, STP®, SLICK-50® or carnauba wax. If you want slicker bullets, buy and load the high-priced spread, moly-coated bullets. Don't tumble loaded rounds of ammunition in any liquid (especially lacquer thinner) to remove the case lube. Lacquer thinner will kill the primers, and tumbling will change the burning rate of your powder (kaboom!). Don't use your cleaning rod like a violinist playing "Flight of the Bumblebee." You may just as well be using a coping saw on your bore. Never plug your bore during storage. It's too easy to forget and blow a barrel, possibly hurting someone!

THINGS TO DO

TAKE THE TIME NECESSARY TO DO A COMPLETE AND THOROUGH JOB OF CLEANING. Take the time to correctly condition the bore of your firearms. Recently, ArmaLite sent out a service bulletin on their AR-10T®, in which they stressed "breaking in the barrel." They recommend a 200 round break-in period. Maybe they know some-thing about the barrels we don't know, but, in most cases, a 100 round break-in will do. It's time consuming, but it pays dividends. They recommend firing and cleaning thoroughly with J-B Non-Imbedding Bore Paste® (10 to 20 strokes) after each of the first 30 shots, after each 3 shots for the next 30, after each five for the next 40, and so on. A little trick I picked up from Mike Bykowski is to coat the bore (wet patch) with Smith & Wesson's "Friction-Block®" after cleaning and before firing the next shot, while doing the break-in. It helps! My AR-15 based match rifle doesn't give me any removable jacket fouling, and neither do three of my other "high-priced" match barrels. If at all possible, store your firearms uncased, with the muzzle facing down, or angling down. It keeps the fluids out of the action and stock and allows air circulation.

Cryo-treating barrels: It makes them last longer, but does not necessarily improve the accuracy. As "Boots" Obermeyer once said, "Cryo-treating a barrel may marginally improve the accuracy of a mediocre bore, but it has relatively little effect on a good one." It has proven to increase life, but at what cost? If you are dealing with a high-intensity cartridge, it may increase barrel life by up to 50%. On a "Swift", perhaps, or a .22/250 Ackly Improved, but how many of us abuse barrels to that extent?

If you're having a quality barrel screwed on a "business rifle", pay the extra money to have the action gone through and "squared." I've run across factory production rifles that could have been used to shoot around corners. One had the receiver ring 15 degrees out of "square" with the centerline of the action and the bore. This particular one couldn't hit the broad side of a barn from the inside. Bolt lug bearing surfaces are another often overlooked factor. Recently, we encountered a bolt that was bearing only 40% on the locking recesses. It, too, benefited from an "action job."

*NOTE: Always let solvents "work" for at least several minutes before wiping them out. They work by chemical action, and just wiping them on and wiping them off immediately does not allow them the time they need to do the job.

Care, Cleaning & Sportsmanship

In conclusion, you don't have to re-invent the wheel. On the other hand, there really are no short cuts when the goal is getting the most accuracy and life out of your favorite firearm.

Again, take the time required to do the job right, and use the equipment to do the job. There are no short-cuts.

CHAPTER SEVEN

Sportsmanship

One of the juniors left a note on my hut at Camp Perry saying he hoped I would address "Cheating" in my section on sportsmanship. He said he sees a lot of it going on. I wanted to talk to him directly, but I'll have to answer here. Before we begin, we must first define our terms.

All cheating is breaking the rules, but not all breaking the rules is cheating. The best example is, all collies are dogs, but not all dogs are collies. The guy shooting a miss, who then fires an extra round, is a cheater. The guy who placed his elbow on his ammo pouch was using artificial support, but he had been shooting three years and no one had ever told him about artificial support. Was he cheating? I don't think so. He just needed to be educated.

Have We Given Up?

In the "Old" days people talked about: Honor, Duty, Integrity, Sportsmanship, and the list goes on. Society did not put up with a liar, a cheater, a murderer, a rapist, etc... These miscreants were exposed, dealt with and/or ostracized. Today we "accept" movies that glorify the bad traits in people, we "allow" ourselves to be told not to be judgmental. We, as a society, have abdicated our responsibilities, allowing "The Law" or someone else to handle it. We don't want to make a scene or bring any attention to ourselves.

Like the man (Edmund Burke?) said: "The only thing required for evil to triumph is for good men to do nothing." If we are not part of the solution, then we are part of the problem. What can I do without causing a big scene? Simple. Cockroaches do not like the light of day. Shine a little light on the subject and take away the opportunity to cheat. If the person had no intention of cheating in the first place, you may be educating him to the rules and/or the etiquette of the sport.

For example: during slow fire, someone shoots on your target. You can call out to your score keeper: "I did not fire that shot." Make sure you call loud enough to be heard on the next firing point. You may wake up "His" scorekeeper and alert "Him" that everyone around knows. It will reduce any temptation "He" may have about firing an extra round.

Education

Inform a rule violator that what they are doing is not legal in a non-threatening and non-confrontational way. Example: the guy who was placing his elbow on the ammo pouch. I told him "See that NRA referee over there? I know him very well. If he saw you do that he would disqualify you." The competitor was shocked and said he had been shooting three years and no one ever told him. He no longer uses artificial support.

The Team Captain of our State Resident Cheater is his friend and will cover for him. The Team Captain has made public statements that he too would cheat. He knows I keep a close eye on both of them and I don't mind shining a light or two.

When the Rules Encourage Cheating

The NRA rules used to state that if a person loaded more than ten rounds in a rapid fire string the persons score would be disqualified. One of our juniors loaded eleven rounds by mistake and his string was disqualified. He still made the state team, at the bottom rather than his usual first place. He learned a valuable lesson.

The 1997 NRA High Power Rifle Rule book: page 44, rule 14.10 Excessive hits © In rapid fire (6) "If a competitor fires more than the required number of shots, and this is verified by the score keeper (rule 14.3.1(b)), and he has more than ten hits on his target, he will receive the value of the LOW ten hits."

Our State Resident Cheater said "From now on, in all my rapid fire stages I'll just load eleven rounds. If I don't get caught, I'll get the high ten. If I do get caught, I'll get the low ten." If that isn't bad enough, look at it this way: You are shooting next to him and you just shot a knot in the 10 and X ring, but they can find only nine holes. Your target is at half mast marked with insufficient hits.

He is shooting the same caliber and fired eleven hits. His scorekeeper didn't catch it (I know, it's the scorekeeper's job to count the rounds as they are fired, but we all know the reality is, he doesn't always do his job, particularly if he is a new shooter). His target is disked with the eleven hit rule and he gets the high ten. The Range Official rules; "You have insufficient hits and he has excessive hits; you shot on his target." You lose your presumption of a double hit by having all your shots in the 9 & 10 ring. You lose your re-fire, your challenge, ten points and possibly the Match. More importantly, you lose your faith in the system.

What Can You Do?

The squeaky wheel gets the grease. Contact the NRA and demand they change the rule back to being disqualified (*note, it looks like our calls have done some good, the 1999 rule should be changed back to the old way, update: it has been changed back). The rules should not encourage cheating. Any person who can't count to ten, or has his head so far into where the sun doesn't shine, has no business with a loaded firearm in the first place. If it was an honest mistake there is still a price to pay. Stupidity has a price. It will cost: time, money, effort or embarrassment. If a safety violation, it could cost a life!

Human Nature

Sportsmanship is a fascinating study in human nature. We usually think of the "Poor Loser" when we think of sportsmanship, if we think of it at all. What's fascinating is watching the winners. We cannot all be National, State or local champions. The winners have a special talent that deserves respect. It is up to the winners to keep that respect and build on it or lose it by their treatment of other people, i.e., put downs & snide remarks thinly veiled as "Jokes." These people I refer to as "Poor Winners."

Boots Obermayer has won a few National Championships, many State Championships, and tons of local matches. He is used to winning and handles himself extremely well. He has not only earned respect for his shooting ability, but for his treatment of other people. He is a true sportsman and a "Good Winner." Boots is used to winning and its second nature to him. We have a common friend who you would never guess to be "The Match Winner."

The Little Giant

Mark Anderson is a Racine County Deputy Sheriff. He has a lovely wife and two wonderful children. He recently built a new house on the old property and he works long hard hours to provide for his family. Unfortunately, Mark doesn't get to shoot as often as he would like. We get to see him only two or three matches a year. He will not shoot a team match for fear of being called into work and having to inconvenience another shooter.

Care, Cleaning & Sportsmanship

Look up "Nice Guy" in the dictionary and there is Mark's picture. I have never actually seen him give the shirt off his back, but I would not be surprised. Boots and I believe that even the people Mark arrests like him.

Mark's first trip to Camp Perry was put on hold. He was taking his wife's car in for a tune-up when the "accident" occurred. An oncoming car lost a wheel which came straight at him. There was a school bus ahead and to the right and the oncoming car full of kids to his left. Mark ducked just as the tire went through his windshield. The driver couldn't make a get-a-way on just three wheels. He said, "Please don't call the cops, it wasn't my fault. I just forgot to put on the lug nuts." Mark whipped out his badge and said: "This is not your lucky day."

When Mark did make it to Camp Perry, we shared a hut and I got to know him better. We would go places together, like commercial row and to restaurants in town. He refused to go anywhere with me when I wore a particular T-shirt. It said: "I'm with Stupid."

Mark wanted to buy an extra rear sight I had, a Redfield International. During my wild spending spree on commercial row I needed more money so I sold him the sight. He shot for several years and worked his way up to Master scores. At 600 yards, he shot several 197s, 198s and occasional 199s, but he never fired a 200.

On Sept. 6th, 1997 we had a four gun 600 yard match. A person has to use Iron Sights for two of the four matches and CAN use a Scope for the other two matches. Mark shot a 200-9X for his first match with Iron Sights. He fired a 200-7X for his second match, again with Iron Sights. He told Wayne Anderson things were going so well, he wondered if he should not switch to the Scope for the last two matches. Wayne told him, "If it's working, don't fix it." For his third match, Mark got careless and dropped a point for a score of 199-11X. He came back for the fourth and final match with a score of 200-11X (He had never shot a 200 before, but once he found out how easy it was, he just kept on doing it). Boots had his usual 798 with 50 some Xs and we thought he had won again. The surprise of the day was Mark Anderson with a score of 799-38Xs.

At our range all the prize money is split three ways: The State Team, The Junior Program and Fire Arms Tech (a legislative fund for defending our gun rights). We have a cook-out and the food is included as part of the entry fee. Everyone gets fed and talks about the day's events.

As each person came up to congratulate Mark, he smiled and said, "Thank you, I got a new sight." He not only smiled, his eyes were smiling. He was in a daze and he floated. He was a perfect "Gentleman." He handled winning with such grace and dignity, he earned double the normal respect due for shooting a good score.

Mark Anderson is Sportsmanship personified. If you run into him at a match and would like to make your own life a little richer, go up and shake his hand. He may be a little puzzled when you look behind him and wonder: "How does someone, 5'9" tall, cast such a long shadow."

Susan Smith & Sportsmanship

When it was learned that Susan Smith had drowned her two small children, someone said, "It just shows how many bad people there are in the world." I replied, "WRONG, it shows how many good people there are. Remember when she said the kids were stolen? Everyone in town turned out on foot or horseback to search the woods for those children."

Unfortunately, poor sportsmanship is not limited to individuals. A club in a neighboring state holds annual "Leg" matches and has a reputation for "Screwing" with out-of-state shooters. They are the equivalent of Susan Smith in sportsmanship, the ones who are noticed and get all the attention. The bad examples stick out like the proverbial sore thumb and you can't help noticing them.

The other side of the coin is the good people. The guy who loans his $2,000 rifle to a perfect stranger whose gun has broken. The fellow who loans his Kowa scope to the new shooter just getting into the sport. The guy who pulls two targets. The people who teach juniors and new shooters so the sport can survive. This is sportsmanship on a daily basis. We see it so often we fail to recognize it as sportsmanship. Look around and recognize the dozen or so examples of good sportsmanship at each match and your heart will wear a smile.

Teams of Giants

Life (People) has a way of surprising me. Just when you run into one of nature's misfits and your faith in man-kind takes a dip, something happens that not only balances the scales, but far outweighs the negative.

I was helping out on the firing line at our Service Rifle Championship during the "Leg" match when one of my former students came up to me and told me the man on the next target cheated. I told him: "I'm not a match official and you should report it to the Match Director or the Range Officer." He didn't want to do it, so I quietly checked into it and found that the man, in fact, did cheat. He fired his first shot on the wrong target. Since there are no sighters in a "Leg" match, he should have been scored a miss. He buffaloed the junior keeping score and continued to fire ten more rounds for record.

I talked to his Team Captain and told him, "That man will NOT take a Leg medal because of his cheating." The Team Captain asked, "How can we handle this quietly?" I thought to myself "Cockroaches don't like the light of day." I made sure the score card was changed to a miss for the first shot, and the cheater did not place in the metal category.

Respect cannot be demanded, it must be earned. One doesn't "lose" respect; it does not get lost. It dies, a little at a time, or all at once. When it dies, a piece of us dies with it, and our level of faith diminishes. Life has a counter balance. Things happen that not only replace that little bit of diminished faith, but fill the cup once again to the brim. At the end of the DCM (Now CMP) week at Camp Perry they hold an impressive awards ceremony in the base theater. My daughter, Maria noticed that as *each* of the twenty-some dignitaries was introduced and took his place, only Marines, former Marines or the wife of a Marine received applause.

She also noticed that as each individual went up to get his award, the whole audience applauded, but the members of the individual's team stood. Army, Marine Corps, Air Force, Navy, and State Teams each gave their own a standing ovation. The National Trophy Team Match is THE biggest and most prestigious match for the Service Teams. The Army had won the NTT Match. As the members of the Army team walked down to the stage, the entire Army and Marine Corps Teams stood and applauded.

My daughter asked: "Why is the entire Marine Corps Team standing and applauding?" "Respect and Sportsmanship!" I told her. Competition is fierce and the rivalry is great, but once the match is over these two professional teams give each other the respect that has been earned.

The theater was quiet as each member received his award. From two rows behind me in a voice that filled the auditorium, a Gunnery Sergeant said "WAY TO GO, ARMY!" The applause that filled that theater was twice as loud and twice as long as any previous round. That applause was for respect and sportsmanship, not just for the Marine Corps Team, but for the shooting sport as a whole.

A cockroach can sit on one end of the scales and maybe even tip them, but when two teams of giants step on the other end...there's no contest.

APPENDIX A

Seven National Champions

Most of us hold the belief, "Anything a National Champion has to say on shooting (gun cleaning), and I want to hear." We tend to look on them with awe and would never think of actually "Talking" to them. They are really very nice people.

Several years ago I decided to ask each of them "How do you clean your bore?" They are all nice people and helpful, BUT, timing is extremely important. I had to wait until they finished shooting so not to disturb their mental conditioning. I had to catch each one before they left the range.

They each gave short answers and I scribbled like a madman. I cannot read my own writing after ten minutes, so now I'm trying to make heads or tails of it after 18 months.

The Champions

Middleton Tompkins; Six time National Champion. "I use a mixture of 50% Barrel Bright (it's no longer available) and 50% Sweets. Bristle brush, with a patch, a dozen times. A couple of dry patches. Repeat. Use a brush for a jag. If patches come out blue, you have fowling, start over."

G. David Tubb; Eleven times National Champion. "You know I Moly coat? I shoot 150 to 200 rounds without cleaning. I use a bronze brush and Shooters Choice, scrub 15-20 times then dry patch. Re-foul the barrel with at least three rounds."

Mitchell Maxberry; 1994 and 1995 National Champion. (Mitch does not Moly coat). "I dip a bronze brush in Hoppes #9 and scrub the bore 10-15 strokes. Dry patch. If there is roughness in the throat, I use Remclean or JB bore cleaner."

Thomas Whitaker; 1996 National Champion. "I really believe in keeping my bore clean. I run 2 or 3 wet patches of Shooters Choice. I then run a wet bronze brush, again with Shooters Choice, about 5 or 6 times. Dry patch. I then use Sweets on a wool mop. Pull through to the muzzle. Let sit a couple minutes. Dry patch. Repeat with Sweets until the patch stops coming out blue. Damp Shooters Choice for storage." Note: I can't read my writing, but he mentions ISSO Bore cleaner, a paste bore cleaner.

Noma Zinsmaster; Woman's National Champion (I don't know how many times). "I use a degreaser called King Colbalt, but I can't get it anymore. I run a few patches with it, then I use Shooters Choice, patches only, I never brush. I then dry patch it. On occasion I use JB Bore cleaner."

Sandy Pagel; 1995 and 1996 Woman's National Champion. "OH, MY GOD—ME? You know I work for Outers. I use their 'Foaming Super Solvent.' I spray it in the bore and let it sit for 10-15 minutes. Dry patch 2 or 3 times, repeat if necessary."

And The Winner Is ---

Nancy Tompkins-Gallagher; (She's married to Mid Tompkins). 1998 National Champion and many, many times Woman's National Champion. "I just give it to Mid."

APPENDIX B

Off the Reservation

Charlie won't give a kind word to anything that isn't tried and true. When one of these new-fangled products have been around a hundred years or so, he'll consider looking at it. None of that is true, but I like saying it.

I'm going "Off the Reservation," on my own and recommending a product that is fairly new. Boots, Jack, Charlie nor Mike have used it and have no opinion one way or the other.

The product is the "Otis Gun Cleaning System (315-942-5484)." They have many products, but the one I and a few friends have tested is the "Universal" Kit. It is contained in a cordura pouch a little larger than a ladies compact. It can be worn on a belt or carried in a jacket pocket.

The Universal kit will clean rifles, shotguns and pistols, anywhere from .22 cal. up to 10 gauge. The best feature of the Otis system is all the firearms can be cleaned from the breech to the muzzle without any disassembly. The rod is a flexible cable. It looks like an airplane control cable, covered in plastic. They call it an "Exclusive nylon bonded steel "Memory Flex" rod." You simply run the cable into the bore from the breech end through the ejection port, open the bolt and slide it in.

The kit comes with three lengths of rods. There is an adapter to connect them for long shotguns. The end of the rod has a special tip to clear the bore of mud, snow, stuck bullets, etc... I keep a rod wrapped in a coil in the pocket of my shooting stool. During a team match, one of my shooters had a stuck bullet when he opened the bolt and the case pulled free. The Otis rod works "*As Advertised.*"

The reason it can clean rifles, pistols and shotguns, from .22 cal. to 10 gauge is the specially designed patch. It is about three inches in diameter and has a series of cuts or slots in certain places. You follow the directions for the cal. of firearm you are cleaning. Place the slotted patch holder in the appropriate cut then pinch the patch at the correct "Clock Position" and fold the patch back onto itself.

One of the clock positions will give you a long narrow patch for the .22 cal. rim fire. Another clock position will give you a shorter and fatter patch for a .30 cal. center fire. Attach the special plug and the patch is ready for a shotgun. You can use each patch up to six times. They make a special kit just for the AR's. See the source list for ordering information.

I am not recommending this kit as your primary gun cleaning method, nor the "memory Flex" as your primary rod. It is an excellent product for hunters to carry into the field. It is being marketed for the military; again for carrying into the field and to get them to clean from the breech to the muzzle (less chance to damage the crown). This is simply another tool for your gun cleaning arsenal.

Update 2015

I am now carrying a new line of cleaning products on my web site: www.JarHeadTop.com
E-mail: Top@Jarheadtop.com Phone 334-347-0020.

BORE TECH, INC. ELIMINATOR™

BTCE-25004
ELIMINATOR BORE CLEANER 4 OZ
$13.99 + S&H

BTCE-25016
ELIMINATOR BORE CLEANER 16 OZ
$34.99 + S&H

BORE TECH, INC. ELIMINATOR™

Bore Tech's ELIMINATOR™ is the patent pending bore cleaner that has taken the shooting industry by storm. As a result of advanced chemical research, ELIMINATOR surpasses the rigorous demands of the modern day shooter and is environmentally safe.

<u>*ELIMINATOR™ QUICKLY REMOVES:*</u>
<u>*CARBON   COPPER   LEAD   CORROSVE RESIDUE*</u>
<u>*ELIMINATOR™ IS 100%*</u>
<u>*BARREL SAFE   ODOR FREE   NON HAZARDOUS*</u>
<u>*BIODEGRADABLE*</u>

ELIMINATOR's proprietary formulation is accomplished

Care, Cleaning & Sportsmanship

through a new combination of chemicals never before introduced to the shooting industry. **ELIMINATOR** has the ability to simultaneously cut through the layers of carbon and copper fouling that have accumulated on the barrel's wall with each shot fired.

ELIMINATOR begins its assault on fouling by chemically loosening and releasing carbon deposits from the barrel's surface. **ELIMINATOR** utilizes a blend of chemical surfactants that break-up and remove carbon deposits with ease. No tedious brushing and patching needed, even on stubborn build-up.

In a two-step process, **ELIMINATOR** first breaks down the copper by reconfiguring its electronic state. Then, by a specially developed binding agent, **ELIMINATOR** acts like a magnet and selectively attracts and captures the copper in a suspended form rendering it unable to redeposit in the firearms bore. The continued rapid and complete extraction of any remaining carbon and copper progresses and cleans unimpeded, undiluted, full strength without becoming saturated with carbon and copper molecules.

<u>Another benefit of **ELIMINATOR** is it also contains a rust preventative</u>, which shields and conditions the firearm's bore after cleaning. Just dampen your last patch with **ELIMINATOR** and your bore is protected from rust and corrosion.

Whether your barrel is steel, stainless steel, or lined, **ELIMINATOR** is **100% SAFE** for an infinite period of time.

Bore Tech's **ELIMINATOR** is without a doubt the premier, state of the art bore cleaner that quickly eliminates carbon and copper fouling without the hazards, toxicity, and odors found in competitive based cleaners. You can trust Bore Tech to put this much attention and detail into a product.

Product Directions:
- ** FIRST UNLOAD FIREARM **
    1. Wet 3 to 4 patches with **ELIMINATOR** and push through bore to remove loose fouling. Only push patches through the bore in **ONE** direction.

2. Next, make 10 to 15 passes with a tight fitting **NYLON** brush saturated with **ELIMINATOR**.
3. Then repeat step 1 and let **ELIMINATOR** soak 3 to 5 minutes.
4. Finally, push dry patches through the bore until they come out clean.
5. Before storing firearm, dampen a patch with **ELIMINATOR** and push through bore.
6. Before using firearm, always run a dry patch through the bore. This will remove any residue and ensure against obstructions.

BORE TECH - C4 CARBON REMOVER

BTCC-35004
C4 CARBON REMOVER 4 OZ
$10.99 + S&H
(That is $2.75 per oz)

BTCC-35016
C4 CARBON REMOVER 16 OZ
$20.99 + S&H
(That is $1.31 per ounce)

Technologically advanced, 100% biodegradable formula is environmentally safe, yet strong enough to remove the toughest carbon, lead, and moly fouling in just seconds. Ideal for rifle barrels, bolt faces, flash suppressors, compensators, silencers, chamber throats, revolver cylinders, gas pistons and any other place extreme carbon fouling is found. Will also neutralize and remove corrosive salts found in surplus military ammunition and black powder. Deep cleaning action easily penetrates the smallest crevices and other hard-to-reach areas, leaving heavily fouled parts looking factory new. For really stubborn fouling just soak in C4 Carbon Remover for a few minutes, then wipe or patch dry. Conditions the metal to help prevent future build-up. Non-flammable, odorless, ammonia free solution is safe for indoor use.

Use Instructions:

- ** FIRST UNLOAD FIREARM **
    1. Wet 3 to 4 patches with **C_4 CARBON REMOVER** and push through bore to remove loose fouling. Only push patches through the bore in **ONE** direction.
    2. Next, make 10 to 15 passes with a tight fitting brush saturated with **C_4 CARBON REMOVER.**
    3. Then, repeat Step 1 and let **C_4 CARBON REMOVER** soak 5 to 10 minutes.
    4. Finally, push dry patches through the bore until they come out clean.
    5. Before storing firearm, dampen a patch with **C_4 CARBON REMOVER** and push through bore.
    Before using firearm, always run a dry patch through the bore. This will remove any residue and ensure against obstructions.

Jim Owens

BORE TECH - CU+2 COPPER REMOVER™

BTCU-26004
CU+2 COPPER REMOVER 4 OZ
$10.99 + S&H

BORE TECH, INC. Cu+2 COPPER REMOVER™

Cu+2 COPPER REMOVER is the brand new patent pending bore cleaner that surpasses the rigorous demands of the modern day shooter and an environmentally minded society. Through advanced chemical research, Cu+2 COPPER REMOVER not only cleans copper fouling faster than any traditional petro-ammonia solvents, it is also 100%

BARREL SAFE
ODOR FREE
AMMONIA FREE
NON HAZARDOUS
BIODEGRADABLE
PETROLEUM FREE

Cu+2 COPPER REMOVER's proprietary formulation and cleaning process is designed for one thing, continued, rapid and complete extraction of any copper fouling in your firearm's bore. The key to the copper removing properties is found in a unique and rapid two-step process. In the first step, the breakdown of the copper is achieved by reconfiguring the copper's electronic state. Metallic copper with a neutral charge, CuO, is oxidized or broken down to its cupric state, Cu+2. Then in the second step, a specially enhanced binding agent within Cu+2 acts like a magnet, and selectively attracts and captures the copper, rendering it unable to redeposit in the firearms bore. In "shooters" terms, instantaneous blue patches and a clean barrel.

Cu+2 COPPER REMOVER also contains a rust preventative, which shields and condition the firearm's bore after cleaning. Just dampen your last patch with **Cu+2 COPPER REMOVER** and your bore is protected from rust and corrosion.

Whether your barrel is steel, stainless steel, or lined, **Cu+2 COPPER REMOVER** is 100% safe for an infinite period of time.

BORE-TECH's Cu+2 COPPER REMOVER is without a doubt the premier, state of the art copper remover that quickly eliminates copper fouling without the hazards, toxicity, and odors found in competitive based cleaners.

Directions:
- ** FIRST UNLOAD FIREARM **
    1. Wet 3 to 4 patches with Cu+2 COPPER REMOVER and push through bore to remove loose fouling. Only push patches through the bore in ONE direction.
    2. Next, make 10 to 15 passes with a tight fitting NYLON brush saturated with Cu+2 COPPER REMOVER.
    3. Then, repeat Step 1 and let Cu+2 COPPER REMOVER soak 3 to 5 minutes.
    4. Finally, push dry patches through the bore until they come out clean.
    5. Before storing firearm, dampen a patch with Cu+2 COPPER REMOVER and push through bore.
    6. Before using firearm, always run a dry patch through the bore. This will remove any residue and ensure against obstructions.

Jim Owens

BORE TECH - BORE TECH MOLY MAGIC

BTCM-15004
MOLY MAGIC 4 OZ
$13.99 + S&H

Bore Tech's **MOLY MAGIC** is a unique blend of penetrants and surfactants formulated exclusively to assist in the removal of molybdenum disulfide buildup in rifle bores.

Molybdenum disulfide (commonly referred to as "Moly") is a substantive material, which means that it clings to metal surfaces readily, and while this is part of the mechanism which allows moly to provide friction reduction, it also makes it difficult to remove with traditional bore cleaning solvents.

In the presence of high temperatures and high pressures, moly breaks down, causing a thick build-up and a corrosive sulfuric acid byproduct. Both residues can significantly decrease accuracy and destroy barrel steel if not appropriately cleaned.

Bore Tech's **MOLY MAGIC** penetrates deep into the metal's pores while a specially formulated surfactant system that suspends and attracts the particles to the patch with electrostatic force, greatly increasing cleaning efficiency. **MOLY MAGIC** is not a bore cleaner, and should be used in conjunction with a bore cleaner like Bore Tech's ELIMINATOR to achieve proper cleaning results.

Care, Cleaning & Sportsmanship

Directions for use:

❏ ** FIRST UNLOAD FIREARM **
1. Clean bore with Bore Tech's **ELIMINATOR™**, following the recommended procedure.
2. Wet 3 to 4 patches with **MOLY MAGIC** and push through bore
3. Next, make 10 to 15 passes with a tight fitting brush saturated with **MOLY MAGIC**.
4. Then repeat step 1 and let **MOLY MAGIC** soak for 10 to 15 minutes.
5. Finally, push dry patches through the bore until they come out clean.
6. If necessary, **MOLY MAGIC** may be left in the bore overnight. It will not damage the bore.
7. Before storing firearm, dampen a patch with Bore Tech's **GUN OIL** or **SHEILD RUST PREVENTATIVE™** and push through bore.

Before using firearm, always run a dry patch through the bore. This will remove any residue and ensure against obstructions.

Jim Owens

BORE TECH - Bore Tech Teflon Gun Oil

BTCO-14004
TEFLON GUN OIL 4 OZ
$10.99 + S&H

Bore Tech's **GUN OIL** is a premium synthetic blend of high purity petroleum based oils, super fine Teflon® fluorocarbon particles, and enhanced rust and corrosion preventing additives designed to offer high performance lubrication and metal conditioning under extreme conditions.

    Displaces Carbon, Moister & Dirt
    Decreases Friction & Wear
    Provides Superior Lubrication & Corrosion Protection
    Prevents Fouling Build-Up & Makes Cleaning Easier

Bore Tech's **GUN OIL** contains a high concentration of pure, sub-micron Dupont® Teflon ideal for treating and protecting metal surfaces. This refined blend offers a superior operating temperature range and will not burn off under extremely high temperatures or become sticky and gummy in the extreme cold. The Bore Tech **GUN OIL** can be applied to *cleaned* metal parts to seal pores with a long lasting coating of Teflon. The enhanced fluoropolymers in **GUN OIL** penetrate and bond deep within the metal's surface preventing carbon, copper and lead fouling buildup. This makes cleaning easier and faster.

Combined with unparalleled corrosion and rust preventatives that effectively displace moister, **GUN OIL** is perfect for any climate or situation.

Care, Cleaning & Sportsmanship

Bore Tech's **GUN OIL** is the right choice for barrels, trigger assemblies, actions, bolts, pistol slides, and any other moving metal parts subjected to extreme elements.

Directions for use:

- ** FIRST UNLOAD FIREARM **
    1. Clean areas to be treated with Bore Tech's **BLAST DEGREASER/CLEANER™** and let dry.
    2. Next, apply **PREMIUM GUN OIL** sparingly to all moving parts. Cycle the parts several times to distribute oil evenly.
    3. If applying to bore, wet a patch/mop and pass through bore.
    4. Before using firearm, always run a dry patch through the bore. This will remove any residue and ensure against obstructions.

PATCHES

Bore Tech's **X-Count™ Patches** are the highest quality, 100% cotton flannel, double napped (on both sides), non-fraying patches money can buy. These patches offer the maximum solvent absorption and cleaning capabilities possible.

X-Count™ Patches come in a variety of square and round sizes to allow proper fit depending on cleaning styles and preferences. All patches are correctly sized to work with **Bore Tech Jags** and other jags.

Patches are packed in re-sealable, hang able, plastic bags for convenience and are available in bags of 100, 250, 500, and 1,000 quantities.

BTPT-118-S100   PATCH 1 1/8" SQUARE 100/Bag for AR-15 $3.69
BTPT-118-S250   PATCH 1 1/8" SQUARE 250/Bag for AR-15 $4.20
BTPT-118-S500   PATCH 1 1/8" SQUARE 500/Bag for AR-15 $6.95
BTPT-118-S1000 PATCH 1 1/8" SQUARE 1000/Bag for AR15 $12.84

JAGS

BTAJ-22-CF
PATCH JAG, .22 CAL CENTERFIRE for AR-15
$5.75 + S&H

Finally an answer to your question, "Is my barrel clean"? Yes, it is **PROOF-POSTIVE** clean.

Bore Tech's revolutionary **PROOF-POSITIVE** jags _eliminate the annoying false indication of copper fouling_ in your bore caused by traditional brass jags. Using a proprietary alloy and secondary treatment process, the new Proof-Positive jags are:

100% Barrel Safe 100% Chemically Resisant
100% Brass Free 100% Heavy Duty

Save your gun from the extremely hard and barrel damaging nickel plated and stainless steel jags.
Rid yourself of the cheap, flimsy and frustrating plastic jags that bend and snap.

Traditional brass jags contain over 60% copper in their composition resulting in the blue copper fouling color on your patch when no copper is present in the bore. By eliminating brass one can effectively determine when a rifle bore is truly copper free and reduce wasted patches, chemical and cleaning time.

Care, Cleaning & Sportsmanship

The Proof-Positive jag line features a proprietary alloy that is as soft as brass but exerts an exceptional tensile strength to prevent bending and snapping under the force of a tight patch.

These jags are specifically engineered to provide superior cleaning and function. Each jag is precision machined to strict tolerances in order to work flawlessly and provide true, concentric pressure on the barrel surface.

When used in conjunction with Bore Tech **BORE STIX**™, a completely edge free transition between the rod and jag results, preventing damage to the firearm's crown when pulling the rod back through the bore.

Nylon Rifle Brush

BTNR-22-003
NYLON RIFLE BRUSH .22 CAL CENTERFIRE for AR-15
$4.49 + S&H

Committed to "setting standards", Bore Tech was the first to recognize the need for quality Nylon Brushes. Bore Tech's double wound **Nylon Brushes** are known for being the finest brushes available. This is due to superior construction and engineered features incorporated into the brush.

Bore Tech's Premium **Nylon Bore Brushes** have twice the amount of bristles compared to the competition, resulting in double the "scrubbing action" and faster cleaning. These brushes feature oversized bristles for extra rigidity and non-brass cores and couplers which prevent the false indication of copper fouling remaining in your bore. This attention to detail is necessary to produce an effective, long lasting, high quality Nylon Bore Brush for your rifle or pistol.

The premium Nylon Brushes are ideal for use with fast acting copper cleaners like Bore Tech's **ELIMINATOR**™ and **CU+2 COPPER REMOVER**™.

BORE TECH - Bore Tech Patch Hog

PATCH HOG
$22.99 + S&H

THE FIRST, THE ORIGINAL, AND STILL THE BEST PATCH AND SOLVENT COLLECTION SYSTEM ON THE MARKET. SIMPLE, NO FUSS, NO MUSS

This is where it all began, with the invention of the **PATCH HOG**. Bore Tech's Patented and revolutionary **PATCH HOG**™ patch and solvent collection system is a unique and safe product developed to eliminate the mess and odors associated with firearm cleaning. The **PATCH HOG** is the answer to fussing with a dirty, smelly trash can or chasing windblown, chemically-saturated patches down range.

The **PATCH HOG** simply slips over the muzzle end of any firearm and securely fastens itself via a non-scratching, thick rubber star washer. No clamps, No straps, No screws required. The **PATCH HOG'S** star washer will grip up to a 2 inch diameter barrel and accommodate most iron sights. The top of the **PATCH HOG** has female threads to accept most standard, plastic water or soft drink bottles.

<u>When the Bore Tech **PATCH HOG** is in place, all of the offensive odors, solvent spray, and dirty patches will be contained when exiting the muzzle. A wet patch never has to be handled.</u>

After cleaning, simply unscrew the used soft drink bottle and dispose of it. No additional cleaning necessary like other manufacturers' products. The Bore Tech **PATCH HOG** is a great gift and is sure to attract attention at the range!

JIM OWENS
www.Jarheadtop.com
Top@jarheadtop.com
Ph 334-347-0020

Appendix C

Source List

Jim Owens, www.JarHeadTop.com
E-mail: Top@Jarheadtop.com
Phone 334-347-0020.

Champion's Choice, Inc. 201 International Blvd., La Vergne, TN 37086
orders 1-800-345-7179

Creedmoor Sports Inc. 167 Creedmoor Way, Anniston, AL 36205
for orders 1-760-757-5529

O. K. Weber, P.O. Box 7485, Eugene, OR 97401 for orders 1-541-747-0458

Sinclair International, 2330 Wayne Haven St., Fort Wayne, IN 46803
Phone 260-493-1858

Brownells, 200 S. Front Street, Montezuma, Iowa 50171
Phone 1-800-741-0015

Master Class Sports (Mo's), 34 Delmar Drive, Brookfield, CT 06804.
Phone 203-775-1013

Fulton Armory, 8725 Bollman Pl. #1 Savage, MD 20763
Phone 301-490-9485

ABOUT THE AUTHOR

Jim's been involved in High Power Competitive Shooting since 1963, winning his first trophy in USMC Boot Camp. During his 23+ years in the Marine Corps, he shot on Base, Wing and Division Teams, served as the NCOIC of MCAS Cherry Point's Small Arms Training Unit -'69-'70, coached on the Marine Corps Rifle Team, MCB Quantico-'81-'83. He coached the winning 6 Man Team in the All USMC Championship Matches in 1983.

Since retiring from the Marine Corps in '86 as a Distinguished Rifleman, Jim has continued his march to excellence in Marksmanship in the civilian arena, becoming a High Master in 1991. He has served on the Board of Directors of the Racine County Line Rifle Club as their High Power Chairman, Military and Police coordinator. He has also served on the Board of Directors of the Wisconsin Rifle and Pistol Association, the last two years as Vice President. (He swears that "Vice" in WI doesn't pay as well as in DC).

Jim has been teaching classes in Marksmanship, safety, and coaching techniques since 1988 and has taken the classes on the road, with classes in IL, OH, TX, KS, NJ, PA, CO & NH.

In 1998 he decided that a web site was in order and with the help of a genuine computer guru, John Klink, he conceived of and delivered his own home page, www.jarheadtop.com, recently described as "the best web site on High Power Shooting on the net".

Jim is a certified NRA Rifle-Pistol –Range Safety Officer and NRA Referee. He is a life member of the "Marine Corps Distinguished Shooters Association" and a life member of the VFW.

Jim currently gives classes on his home range in Enterprise, AL.

For more info on Jim's classes, visit the web site or call Jim at: 334-347-0020

Shooting Products from Jim Owens

Sight Alignment, Trigger Control & The Big Lie

A Power-packed book that has helped many shooters improve their groups and scores, some by as much as forty or fifty points. This book covers not only the basics of breathing, natural point of aim, sight alignment, sight picture, focus and trigger control exercises. It has sections on Mental conditioning, marking the sights, zeroing, normal come ups, light effects, damage to the crown, care in cleaning, throat erosion and bullet run out. There is also an advanced theory that has been praised by High Masters and Marksmen.
- *Now in Paperback & Ebook versions -*

New CD version includes a new chapter **"Analyzing Groups"** with more and better pictures for the price of the book. Yes, you may print off pages as you need them for the range!
$14.95 plus $2.80 S&H

Reading the Wind and Coaching Techniques

To excel in any outdoor shooting sport you will need to learn how to compensate for the effects of the wind. Jim Owens' 20+ years of Marine Corps Shooting Team experience will give you the knowledge of how to read, judge and adjust for the wind—in any type of rifle competition.

You'll learn a simple system for judging the speed, direction and value of the wind. You'll learn to read the mirage, how to accurately read the range flag, estimate wind speed, wind strategies, effects on the bullet and much more. Also included are 22 sets of wind charts for a variety of calibers (.223, .308, 6.5-08, 6.5-284, .300 Win. Mag.), bullet weights, and for **both** Across the course and Long Range. 80 wind charts in total!
- *In Ebook & Paperback (Jan. 2015) versions -*

Now on CD too, in an easy to use PDF format, more and better pictures for the price of the book. Yes, you may print off pages as you need them for the range!
$12.95 plus $2.80 S&H

The Leather Sling and Shooting Positions

Learn to assemble the leather sling in the same method taught by the Marine Corps Team. Follow a four-step program to shooting positions, the likes of which you have never seen before. As an added bonus, receive a five-step theory that could increase your off-hand three to ten points.

Now on CD, with a new chapter on the **No-Pulse Sling**, with more and better pictures for the price of the book. Yes, you may print off pages as you need them for the range!
$12.95 plus $2.80 S&H
 - *Also in Ebook & Paperback*

"Four Book Set"

Get all four books at a special reduced rate! *Save $5.85*
"Reading the Wind and Coaching Techniques", "Sight Alignment, Trigger Control and the Big Lie", "Leather Sling and Shooting Positions", "Care, Cleaning and Sportsmanship"

All four together on CD-rom, with all the added chapters and wind charts from each individual book as well as all the newer and better pictures!
$43.95 plus $5.40 S&H

Advance Theory CD

For many years shooters have made a sight adjustment and have come out the other side. Someone would tell them, "you must put one click on the rifle and one click in your head". The "Windage and Elevation" rule states, "One click will move the strike of the bullet one inch per 100 years. Jim's Advance Theory says, You must do two things with it: (1) Memorize it, because people will talk about it, and (2) Forget it, it does not work!
Jim gives you an alternate theory in three Power Point Presentations on the CD - That Does Work!
And, get Personal Support after viewing the CD! If you have any questions or do not understand something, just call Jim at 334-340020 and he will be more than happy to help you.
$20 plus $2.20 S&H

Reading The Wind 2 CD Set

The first CD has Jim's "*Reading the Wind*" that he uses in his classes; the most recent and best efforts.
Included:

- Different forces affecting the bullet
- A simple system anyone can use to "Read The Wind"
- Simple and inexpensive aides to help you
- A detailed description as to reading the mirage
- A simple and the most accurate way to read flags
- "Alternative" methods when the mirage or flags are not readable

The second CD has 22 Sets of really good Wind Charts - PLUS a bonus short class on using Kentucky Windage.
$25 plus $3.50 S&H

Line & Pit Procedures CD

When we 1st participate in a new sport we are a little intimidated. We don't know what to expect. We do not want to make a mistake, look foolish, maybe having someone yell at us or mess someone else up.

Well, come along with me. We are going to a High Power Rifle Match. We are going from start to finish. From the time we arrive at the Range, to checking in at the stat office, getting assigned our relay, dropping our gear off at the ready line and reporting to the Pits. •We are going to be there all day. We will see the different relays fire the Match and in turn see the different problems that can come up and how they are handled. •We are going to find out where to go and when. We will find out what we have to do when we get there and what supplies we will need. We will find out the proper way to run a target, both in slow fire and rapid fire. How to handle the different situations. •We will learn the Range Commands, both Line and The Pits. We will learn the flow of the Match.

I am going to show you some of the small tricks I have learned in over 45 years of shooting. **$11.95 plus $2.20 S&H**

Score Keeping CD

You learn by doing! After the instruction phase you actually score a shooter in both slow fire and rapid fire. The different problems that can occur will be presented as you score the shooter. You will get years of experience in a single setting. In fact, you will know more than most people that have been shooting 5 to 10 years.
$11.95 plus $2.20 S&H

The Complete AR-15 High Performance Guide

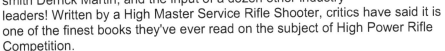

The latest on accuracy modifications and accessories for "Space Guns" and Service Rifles. It features an extensive hand loading section and shooting techniques specifically suited to the AR-15. It also includes special chapters with 11-time Champion G. David Tubb on the AR-10/SR-25; US-AMU head C.I. Boyd and ace shooter Sgt. Lew Tippie; gunsmith Derrick Martin; and the input of a dozen other industry leaders! Written by a High Master Service Rifle Shooter, critics have said it is one of the finest books they've ever read on the subject of High Power Rifle Competition.

$28.95 plus $5.40 S&H

Hand loading for Competition

A brand new book by the author and publisher of The Competitive AR15. It's a guide to "practical precision" in producing high-performance ammunition.

$ 34.95 plus $5.40 S&H

Jim Owens Data Book

Some of the features are Eight Sets of Wind Charts, A Wind Speed Estimating Guide, More than Twice the # of pages., Larger plotting areas, All Scoring rings are Proportional, Jim Owens "Amended" grid lines, Twin plotting bulls for rapid fire, A "Gun Round Count" page, A Check list for items to bring to the range, A chart detailing the scores needed for each classification, A chart giving the dimensions of the scoring rings, A chart describing the scoring system, A guide for normal come-ups from 100 to 1,000 yards in 100 yard increments, A chart explaining the "9-Yes, 9-No" problems. This data book is more than a $60.00 value.

$15.95 Plus $5.40 S&H. Sent via Priority Mail

NEW - Use of the Jim Owens Data Books

$15.00 plus S&H or $10.00 plus S&H if ordered with any data book!

Jim Owens (Long Range) Data Book

Some of the features are: 54 two sided pages for the 600 yard stage and 54 two sided pages for the 800/900/1,000 yard target, 14 Sets of Wind Charts, A Wind Speed Estimating Guide, Larger plotting areas, All Scoring rings are Proportional, Jim Owens "Amended" grid lines, A "Gun Round Count" page, A chart detailing the scores needed for each classification, A chart giving the dimensions of the scoring rings, A chart describing the scoring system, A guide for normal come-ups from 100 to 1,000 yards in 100 yard increments.
$15.95 Plus $5.40 S&H. Sent via Priority Mail

Contact me at:

Jim Owens
112 Red Wing Dr.
Enterprise, AL 36330
334-347-0020
Top@JarHeadTop.com
www.JarHeadTop.com

What they are saying about
Sight Alignment, Trigger Control & The Big Lie

"My scores have improved drastically. I thank you for your books. High Power shooting is enjoyable when you do better."
—Neal Trubitt

"After shooting my first match a few weeks ago. One of the guys from my club loaned me a set of your books. I can not thank you enough. I can understand what you are talking about. I know the next match will go much better for me. Thanks Again"
—John DeMoss

"Your series of books and tapes have helped me make the first daunting steps and I entered my first competitive event ever, the 2004 NRA High Power Week Competition at Camp Perry. Your Data Book is the best that I have seen and all the information that you had put together and your personal commitment to Juniors in the sport is indeed commendable."
—Steven Field

"Your books were so great and helpful, I gave them to my Dad, and have not seen them back! So I need another set!"
—Another happy customer

Made in the USA
Lexington, KY
09 November 2017